PORTUGUESE:
AN ESSENTIAL GRAMMAR

PORTUGUESE: AN ESSENTIAL GRAMMAR

Amélia P Hutchinson and Janet Lloyd

London and New York

First published 1996
by Routledge
11 New Fetter Lane, London EC4P 4EE

Simultaneously published in the USA and Canada
by Routledge
29 West 35th Street, New York, NY 10001

© Amélia P. Hutchinson and Janet Lloyd 1996

Typeset in Times by Florencetype Ltd, Stoodleigh, Devon
Printed and bound in Great Britain by
Clays Ltd, St Ives plc

British Library Cataloguing in Publication Data
A catalogue record for this book is available from the British Library

Library of Congress Cataloguing in Publication Data
Hutchinson, Amélia P., 1949–
Portuguese: an essential grammar/Amélia P. Hutchinson and Janet Lloyd.
(Essential grammar)
Includes index.
1. Portuguese language – Grammar. 2. Portuguese language – Textbooks for foreign
speakers – English. I. Lloyd, Janet, 1968–. II. Title. III. Series.
PC5067.3.H88 1996
469.82'421–dc20 96–36

ISBN 0–415–13707–1 (hbk)
        0–415–13708–X (pbk)

CONTENTS

PART III: BRAZILIAN VARIANTS

1–11   Brazilian essential grammar

FOREWORD

The aim of this work is to offer the student of Portuguese a succinct and reasonably comprehensive overview of Portuguese grammar.

We have attempted to cater for different groups of students, each with their own needs: the beginner, who may not have an extensive knowledge of grammatical concepts and terminology yet requires a guide through the grammar of the language; the intermediate–advanced student, who appreciates a clear reference book in moments of doubt; and the independent or adult learner, who is studying Portuguese not for academic purposes but with other aims in mind, such as business or travel.

Above all, we have aimed to produce a 'user-friendly' handbook with concise explanations of areas of grammar and comprehensible examples taken from current Portuguese usage. This latter point is significant, given our firm belief that grammar should not stand divorced from usage. Nevertheless, the 'essential' nature of this work means that we have been obliged to use short illustrative phrases or sentences out of context.

We have tried to make the book as 'neutral' as possible, bearing in mind the differences between European Portuguese, Brazilian Portuguese and the Portuguese spoken in the Lusophone African countries. Although we have taken European Portuguese as our starting-point, we have indicated the most marked differences between this and Brazilian grammar and usage in Part III. We have aimed, thus, to cover both ends of the spectrum. As African Portuguese falls somewhere between these two extremes with divergences which are more lexical than grammatical, we have decided not to extend this work into that area.

Part II which deals with language functions was largely inspired by National Curriculum guidelines for other languages. In this way, we have also endeavoured to address the needs of teachers of Portuguese in secondary education.

If, with this product of our effort, we can assist a wider range of people in learning and developing their knowledge of Portuguese, the eighth most spoken language in the world, we will consider ourselves well rewarded.

Acknowledgements

We are grateful to many colleagues for their advice and assistance (and, in some cases, patience) in the writing of this book. Our sincere thanks go to members of the Spanish and Portuguese section of the Department of Modern Languages, University of Salford, and especially to Professor Leo Hickey, for his observations, which helped us to avoid many glaring mistakes; to Mr Malcolm Marsh for his advice on how to illustrate pronunciation and to Ms Cristina Sousa, for her helpful comments regarding language functions. We would also like to single out Dr Mike Harland of the University of Glasgow for his very welcome encouragement and Mr Carlos Sachs of the University of Manchester for his advice on Brazilian Portuguese usage.

Our thanks also go to Mr Peter Bull of William Hulme's Grammar School, Manchester, and Mr Neville Mars of St Edward's College, Liverpool for their support in this venture. Likewise, we are also grateful to Dr John Rae, Director of the Enterprise in Higher Education Unit of the University of Salford, and Mr Andrew Hollis of the Department of Modern Languages, University of Salford.

Many more people, British students of Portuguese and Portuguese postgraduate students of the University of Salford, offered their kind and enthusiastic support in the form of suggested examples or spontaneous comments frequently elicited by our dynamic collaborator, Maria José Azevedo Silva, whose role was of intrinsic value during the earlier stages of this project, the work having been initiated by Rute Franco Camacho.

Obviously, we could not overlook the contribution of our students, who, over the years, have offered themselves as guinea pigs and their comments have always been most welcome.

Despite the care that has gone into producing this book, there are, no doubt, errors, oversights and inaccuracies for which we take full responsibility.

Amélia P. Hutchinson
Janet Lloyd
Salford

HOW TO USE THIS BOOK

Part I covers the fundamental aspects of Portuguese grammar and is intended for reference and illustrative use.

Part II covers a wide range of language functions to assist students in putting grammar into context. In this part, our aim was to present a series of short, self-contained dialogues which not only illustrate language functions but also provide the student and the teacher with useful source texts. The dialogues may be developed in a number of ways, of which we suggest:

(a) role-play;
(b) a starting-point for development of narrative skills;
(c) grammatical analysis;
(d) comprehension exercises.

As we have tried as far as possible to use everyday Portuguese situations in the dialogues, we hope that they may also provide useful cultural references.

Part III presents the main variants of Brazilian Portuguese. Entries in this section carry the prefix 'B' and correspond to chapter and section numbers in Parts I and II. In these parts, superscript capital [B] indicates a Brazilian variant which can be found in Part III.

Most words in the Index are grammatically classified and it is intended as a learning tool. We hope that students who regularly consult the Index will gradually become accustomed to certain grammatical terms, thus finding that explanations in the book become progressively clearer.

PART I: AN ESSENTIAL GRAMMAR

1 PRONUNCIATION AND SPELLING

The following chapter offers a pronunciation guide to European Portuguese with examples of similar sounds in English. Wherever possible, we have attempted to provide close equivalent sounds in English but where this has proved impossible, we offer approximate equivalents.

1.1 VOWELS

1.1.1 Oral vowels

		Example	*Pronounced as*
a	open a	**sap*a*to**	f*a*t
	closed a	**s*a*pato**	*a*bout
	unstressed a	**boc*a***	*a*nnounce
e[B]	open e	**ch*e*que**	ch*e*que
	closed e	**cab*e*lo**	*e*ncounter
	unstressed e	**chequ*e***	bak*e*
	as conjunction, or	*e*	*ee*l
	as first syllable of word	***e*lefante**	
i		**f*i*ta**	f*ee*t
o[B]	open o	**l*o*ja**	l*o*zenge
	closed o	**p*o*ço**	b*oo*k
	unstressed o is pronounced as **u**	**poç*o***	
u[1]		**l*u*ta**	l*oo*t

[1] The **u** is silent in **que, qui, gue** and **gui** (**quente, quinta, guerra, guitarra**) and pronounced in **qua, quo** and **gua** (**quatro, quotidiano, guarda**).

But there are some exceptions where the **u** is read: **tranquilo.**[B]

Note: An acute accent over a vowel means that it is 'open' (e.g. **lá, pé, avó**), whereas a circumflex accent means that the vowel is 'closed' (e.g. **lê, avô**).

1.1.2   Nasal vowels (produced with some nasal resonance)

A vowel is nasal if a *tilde* (~) is written above it or if it is followed by
-m or **-n** within the same syllable:

	Example	*Pronounced as*
ã	**lã**	la*m*b
am	**amplo**	*am*ple
an	**planta**	
em	**empréstimo**	*em*power
en	**entre**	
om	**compras**	co*n*trary
on	**contar**	
im	**sim**	see*n*
in	**tinta**	ti*n*der
um	**tumba**	to*m*b
un	**nunca**	

The word **muito** has a unique pronunciation because the **i** is pronounced
as a nasal vowel.

1.2   CONSONANTS[B]

Most Portuguese consonants are pronounced in the same way as their
English equivalents, except for:

	Example	*Pronounced as*
ç[1]	**laço**	la*c*e
ch	**champu**	*sh*ampoo
g + a,o,u[2]	**gás**	*g*ash
g + e, i	**gelo**	mea*s*ure
h	**hora**	(not pronounced)
j	**já**	mea*s*ure
lh	**milhão**	mi*ll*ion
nh	**vinho**	o*ni*on
q[3]	**quadro**	*q*uack

[1] **c** is pronounced as in 'la*c*e' before **e** and **i**, and as in '*c*at' before **a**, **o** and **u**. To be
pronounced as in 'la*c*e' before **a**, **o** and **u**, it must have a cedilla: **ç**.

[2] **u** after **g** is silent, when followed by **e** or **i** (e.g. **guitarra**, **guerra**).

[3] **q** appears only before **u**. Normally, the **u** is silent if **e** or **i** follow (e.g. **máquina**).

r

intervocalic or final, or preceded by a consonant (except **n** or **l**)	**pa*r*ar** **comp*r*as**	p*r*ete*r*ite (rolling the 'r')
initial, or preceded by **n** or **l**	**rabo** **ten*r*o** **mel*r*o**	*R*obbie (with Scottish pronunciation)

rr

	ca*rr*o	(as initial 'r')

s

initial	**samba**	*s*amba
intervocalic, or final if followed by vowel	**casa** **meu*s* amigos** }	ka*s*bah
at end of syllable/word, if followed by unvoiced consonant (**t, c, f, p**)	**vesta** **mosca** **fó*s*foros** **meu*s* pais** }	*s*ugar
at end of syllable/word, if followed by voiced consonant (**b, d, g, m, n, r**)	**Lisboa** **há*s*-de** **ra*s*gar** **me*s*mo** **ci*s*ne** **I*s*rael** **a*s* mãos** }	mea*s*ure

x

usual pronunciation	**xerife** **México** **peixe** **excelente**	*sh*eriff me*sh* fi*sh* g*eish*a
in words beginning with **ex-** plus vowel	**exame** **existir** **exótico** }	ea*s*y
in a few words (memorize!)	**taxi** **tórax**	ta*x*i thora*x*
in still fewer words (memorize!)	**trouxe** **próximo**	*s*ing Pro*ss*er

z

initial, or intervocalic	**zebra** **dizer**	*z*ebra de*ss*ert
final	**luz**	lou*ch*e

1.3   DIPHTHONGS

1.3.1   Oral diphthongs

	Example	Pronounced as
ai	**p***ai*	p*ie*
au	**m***au*	p*ow*er
ei[1]	**l***ei*	l*ay*
eu[1]	**t***eu*	*Eu*phrates (with the 'e' pronounced as the 'i' in 'it')
iu	**part***iu*	*Eu*rope
oi[1]	**f***oi*	'*oy*ez!'
ou	**s***ou*	th*ough*
ui	**f***ui*	Lo*ui*siana (with more emphasis on the 'u')

[1] When these diphthongs carry an acute accent, the first vowel is pronounced with its equivalent open sound (see 1.1.1). E.g. **papéis**, **chapéu**, **sóis**.

1.3.2   Nasal diphthongs[B]

	Example	Pronounced as
ãe	**m***ãe*	m*ai*n (approx.)
ãi	**c***ãi***bra**	C*ai*n (approx.)
ão	**p***ão*	p*ou*nd (but more nasal)
-am	**am***am*	m*ou*nd (but more nasal)
-em, **-en**(s)	**s***em*	s*ai*nt (approx.)
	parab*éns*	ch*ai*n (approx.)
õe	**p***õe*	b*oi*ng (approx.)

1.4   STRESS

Portuguese words are normally stressed on the penultimate syllable, or on the final syllable if ending in **-r**, **-l**, **-z** or **-u**. In these cases, the accent is not required:

do-cu-*men***-to**	document
ve-*lu***-do**	velvet
pro-fes-*sor*	teacher
ti-*rar*	take
co-*mer*	eat
par-*tir*	brake
pa-*pel*	paper
a-*zul*	blue

ca-*paz*	capable
fe-*liz*	happy
pe-*ru*	turkey

But whenever the stress falls on the antepenultimate or last syllable, other than in the cases indicated above, the word has to take an accent:

úl-ti-mo	last
cha-mi-*né*	chimney
ir-*mã*	sister
fú-til	futile
mó-vel	piece of furniture/mobile

1.5   ACCENTS

In Portuguese there are four accents:

- ´ acute accent (opens the vowel): **água**
- ^ circumflex accent (closes the vowel): **Zêzere**
- ~ tilde (nasalizes the vowel): **irmã**
- ` grave accent (used only when there is a contraction of the preposition **a** with an article or pronoun): **àquilo** (**a** + **a** = **à**; **a** + **aquilo** = **àquilo**)

The accent is also used:

(a) to distinguish different words:

pelo	by	**pêlo**	fur; body hair
maça	mace	**maçã**	apple
pela	by, for, through	**péla**	ball

(b) to distinguish verbal forms:

| **compramos** | we buy | **comprámos** | we bought |

2 NOUNS

2.1 GENDER I: MASCULINE AND FEMININE

There are two genders: masculine and feminine. The gender of a noun is determined by its ending, its meaning or its origin.

Note: When you learn new words, always make sure you learn their genders!

2.1.1 The masculine gender is normally used for male persons, animals and professions commonly assigned to males. Most nouns ending in **-o, -l, -r** and **-z** are masculine:

o **pato**	duck	o **colar**	necklace
o **papel**	paper	o **juíz**	judge

2.1.1.1 Also masculine are:

- *Names of oceans, seas, rivers, lakes, capes and mountain ranges*

o **Atlântico**	the Atlantic	o **Lucerna**	Lake Lucerne
o **Báltico**	the Baltic	o **Finisterra**	Cape Finisterre
o **Tejo**	the Tagus	os **Himalaias**	the Himalayas

- *Wines*

o **Porto**	Port	o **Dão**	Dão

- *Cars*

o **Ferrari**	Ferrari	o **Rover**	Rover

- *Names of seasons*

o **Verão**	Summer
o **Outono**	Autumn
o **Inverno**	Winter

But   a **Primavera**   Spring

- *Names of letters*:   o **'a'**; o **'p'**.

- *Cardinal numbers*:   o **um**; o **duzentos**   'one; two hundred'.

But the gender of *ordinal numbers* agrees with that of the noun they correspond to:

o primeiro	minuto	the first	minute
	dia		day
	mês		month
	ano		year
	século		century

| a primeira hora | the first hour |
| a primeira semana | the first week |

- *Words of Greek origin ending in* **-a**

o telegrama	telegram	o clima	climate
o mapa	map	o telefonema	phone call
o cinema	cinema		

2.1.2 The feminine gender is normally used for female persons, animals and professions commonly assigned to females. Most nouns ending in **-a**, **-ã**, **-ade**, **-ice** and **-gem** are feminine:

a panela	pot	a velhice	old age
a irmã	sister	a viagem	journey
a verdade	truth		

But do not forget that there are some words that end in **-a** and are masculine! (See above, 2.1.1.1.)

2.1.2.1 Also feminine are:

- *Names of sciences and arts*

| a Medicina | Medicine | a Arquitectura | Architecture |
| a Matemática | Mathematics | a Pintura | Painting |

- *Days of the week*

a segunda-feira	Monday	a quinta-feira	Thursday
a terça-feira	Tuesday	a sexta-feira	Friday
a quarta-feira	Wednesday		

| *But* | o sábado | Saturday |
| | o domingo | Sunday |

2.1.3 Concrete nouns ending in **-e** and **-ão** are masculine:

| o leite | milk | o limão | lemon |
| *But* a mão | hand | | |

2.1.4 Abstract nouns ending in **-e** and **-ão** are feminine:

a morte   death   **a paixão**   passion

2.2   GENDER II: FORMING THE FEMININE

Nouns ending in	Add	Change into
-o		**-a**
consonant	**-a**	
-or	**-a**	
-or		**-triz**
-or		**-eira**
-eu		**-eia**
-ão		**-ã**
-ão		**-oa**
-ão		**-ona**

2.2.1 Most nouns ending in **-o** form their feminine by changing this ending into **-a**:

o tio   **a tia**   uncle   aunt

2.2.2 Most nouns ending in a consonant or **-or** form their feminine by adding an **-a**:

o português   **a portuguesa**   Portuguese man/woman
o cantor   **a cantora**   singer

But there are two exceptions! See 2.2.2.1 and 2.2.2.2.

2.2.2.1 Nouns ending in **-or** can change into **-triz** (fem.):

o actor   **a actriz**   actor   actress
o embaixador   **a embaixatriz**[1] ambassador   ambassadress

[1] **Embaixatriz** is the wife of the ambassador; *but* if the ambassador happens to be a woman, she is an **embaixadora**.

2.2.2.2 Nouns ending in **-or** can also change into **-eira**:

o lavrador   **a lavradeira**   farmer

2.2.3 Nouns ending in **-eu** form their feminine by changing into **-eia**:

o europeu   **a europeia**   the European

2.2.4 Nouns ending in **-ão** form their feminine by changing into **-ã**, **-oa** or **-ona**:

o anão	a anã	dwarf	
o leão	a leoa	lion	lioness
o solteirão	a solteirona	bachelor	spinster
But o barão	**a baronesa**	baron	baroness

2.2.5 Some nouns have different endings for their masculine and feminine forms:

o consul	a consulesa	consul	
o herói	a heroina	hero	heroine
o poeta	a poetisa	poet	poetess

2.2.6 Some nouns have a common form for both genders.

2.2.6.1 The only thing that varies is the article:

o doente	a doente	patient
o jovem	a jovem	youth
o artista	a artista	artist
o presidente	a presidente	president
o concorrente	a concorrente	competitor/contestant
o intérprete	a intérprete	interpreter
o colega	a colega	colleague
o estudante	a estudante	student
o emigrante	a emigrante	emigrant
o dentista	a dentista	dentist
o turista	a turista	tourist
o jornalista	a jornalista	journalist
o guia	a guia	guide
o futebolista	a futebolista	football player

2.2.6.2 The article remains the same whether it refers to male or female:

a criança	child
a testemunha	witness
o cônjuge	spouse

2.2.7 There are also pairs of words to denote male and female:

o macho	a fêmea	male	female
o cavalo	a égua	stallion	mare
o cão	a cadela	dog	bitch

o bode	a cabra	billy-goat	goat
o carneiro	a ovelha	ram	ewe
o boi	a vaca	ox	cow
o galo	a galinha	rooster	hen
o rapaz	a rapariga	boy	girl
o homem	a mulher	man	woman
o marido	a esposa	husband	wife
o pai	a mãe	father	mother
o padrasto	a madrasta	stepfather	stepmother
o padrinho	a madrinha	godfather	godmother
o genro	a nora	son-in-law	daughter-in-law
o avô	a avó	grandfather	grandmother
o rei	a rainha	king	queen

2.2.8 Some nouns referring to animals have a fixed form and gender regardless of the animal's sex:

o abutre	vulture	**a formiga**	ant
o rouxinol	nightingale	**a foca**	seal
o tigre	tiger	**a raposa**	fox
a cobra	snake		

2.2.8.1 When it is necessary to indicate the natural sex of these animals, the Portuguese equivalent to male (**macho**) and female (**fêmea**) should be used:

| **o abutre fêmea** *or* **a fêmea do abutre** | female vulture |
| **a foca macho** *or* **o macho da foca** | male seal |

Note: Adjectives qualifying these nouns agree with the gender of the noun and not with the gender of the animal:

| **um bonito tigre fêmea** | a beautiful female tiger |
| **uma bonita foca macho** | a beautiful male seal |

2.3   NUMBER: FORMING THE PLURAL

Nouns ending in	*Add*	*Change into*
vowel	-s	
nasal diphthongs	-s	
consonant:		
-n, -r, -s, -z	-es	
-ão		-ões

Nouns ending in	Add	Change into
-ão		-ães
-ão		-ãos
-m		-ns
-al		-ais
-el		-eis
-ol		-ois
-ul		-uis
-il (stressed)		-is
-il (unstressed)		-eis

2.3.1 Nouns ending in a vowel or a nasal diphthong generally form their plural by adding an **-s**:

a mesa	as mesas	table	tables
o jogo[1]	os jogos	game	games
a lei	as leis	law	laws
o chapéu	os chapéus	hat	hats
a mãe	as mães	mother	mothers

[1] Usually, the closed **-o-** sound of the stressed syllable in a word ending in **-o** changes into its equivalent open sound before adding the **-s**:

o jogo	os jogos	game	games
o almoço	os almoços	lunch	lunches
o corpo	os corpos	body	bodies
o ovo	os ovos	egg	eggs
o povo	os povos	people	peoples
o osso	os ossos	bone	bones
o olho	os olhos	eye	eyes
o fogo	os fogos	fire	fires
o imposto	os impostos	tax	taxes

2.3.2 Nouns ending in a consonant (**-n, -r, -s, -z**) form their plural by adding **-es**:

o líquen	os líquenes	lichen	lichens
o professor	os professores	teacher	teachers
o país	os países	country	countries
a luz	as luzes	light	lights

2.3.3 The majority of nouns ending in **-ão** form their plural by changing this ending into **-ões**:

a ambição	as ambições	ambition	ambitions
o coração	os corações	heart	hearts

But a few change into **-ães**:

o pão	**os pães**	bread	loaves of bread
o cão	**os cães**	dog	dogs

and fewer still into **-ãos**!

a mão	**as mãos**	hand	hands
o irmão	**os irmãos**	brother	brothers

2.3.4   Nouns ending in **-m** form their plural by changing into **-ns**:

o som	**os sons**	sound	sounds
a nuvem	**as nuvens**	cloud	clouds

2.3.5   Nouns ending in **-al**, **-el**, **-ol** and **-ul** form their plural by changing into **-ais**, **-eis**, **-ois** and **-uis**:

o animal	**os animais**	animal	animals
o hotel	**os hotéis**	hotel	hotels
o sol	**os sóis**	sun	suns
o paul	**os paúis**	swamp	swamps
But			
o mal	**os males**	evil	evils
o consul	**os consules**	consul	consuls

2.3.6   Nouns ending in stressed **-il** form their plural by changing into **-is**:

o funil	**os funis**	funnel	funnels

2.3.7   *But* nouns ending in unstressed **-il** change into **-eis** in the plural:

o fóssil	**os fósseis**	fossil	fossils

2.3.8   Some nouns ending in **-s** have the same form for both singular and plural:

o lápis	**os lápis**	pencil	pencils
o ourives	**os ourives**	goldsmith	goldsmiths
o cais	**os cais**	quay	quays
o pires	**os pires**	saucer	saucers

2.3.9   Some nouns are almost exclusively used in the plural form:

as algemas	handcuffs	**os óculos**	glasses
as calças	trousers	**os calções**	shorts

2.3.10 Some words have different meanings in the singular and in the plural:

o pai	os pais	father	fathers/parents
o filho	os filhos	son	sons/children
a avó	as avós	grandmother	grandmothers
	os avós		grandparents

2.4   DIMINUTIVES AND AUGMENTATIVES

	Diminutive suffixes	Augmentative suffixes
Fem.	zinha, zita, inha	ona
Masc.	zinho, zito, inho	ão

2.4.1 The Portuguese language uses diminutive and augmentative suffixes to express degrees of size, intensity, affection, etc. Normally, diminutives are used to express smallness, affection and pity, whereas augmentatives usually express largeness, greatness or ugliness.[B]

Diminutives

- smallness   **carrinho**   small car
- affection   **mãezinha**   mummy
- pity   **coitadinho**   poor thing

Augmentatives

- largeness   **carrão**   large car
- greatness   **mulherona**   strong woman
- ugliness   **carão**   ugly face

Note: It is not always possible to translate diminutives or augmentatives into English. *These suffixes can have pejorative or grotesque meanings. They should be used by beginners with caution!*

2.4.2 Diminutives are generally used by children or by adults when talking to children:

A minha amiguinha chama-se Joaninha e anda comigo na escolinha.
My little friend is called Joaninha and she is in my school.

Se comeres a comidinha toda dou-te uma prendinha!
If you eat all this lovely food I'll give you a nice present!

2.4.3 The most common diminutive suffixes are **-zinha**, **-zinho**, **-zita**, **-zito** and **-inha**, **-inho**, **-ita**, **-ito**.[B]

2.4.3.1   **-zinha, -zinho, -zita, -zito** can simply be added to the end of the word:

mamã	+	zinha	=	**mamãzinha**	mummy
móvel	+	zinho	=	**movelzinho**	small piece of furniture
João	+	zinho	=	**Joãozinho**	Johnny
avião	+	zinho	=	**aviãozinho**	little plane
café	+	zinho	=	**cafezinho**	small cup of coffee
viela	+	zita	=	**vielazita**	small alley
pó	+	zito	=	**pozito**	light dust

If the word contains an accent, that accent is dropped unless it is indicating a nasal sound:

pé	+	zito	=	**pezito**	foot
chá	+	zinho	=	**chazinho**	tea
avião[1]	+	zinho	=	**aviãozinho**	little plane

[1] The plural of these words is formed from the normal plural of the word itself before adding **-s**:

avião/aviãozinho	aviões/aviõezinhos
anão/anãozinho	anões/anõezinhos

2.4.3.2   Words ending in **-m** change into **-n** before adding the suffix:

homem	+	zinho	=	**homenzinho**	little man
romagem	+	zinha	=	**romagenzinha**	small pilgrimage
viagem	+	zita	=	**viagenzita**	small trip

2.4.3.3   Words ending in **-s, -z,** only need **-inho** or **-ito** to form a diminutive:

inglês	+	inho	=	**inglesinho**	nice English boy
nariz	+	inho	=	**narizinho**	pretty little nose
rapaz	+	ito	=	**rapazito**	little boy

2.4.3.4   Words ending in **-l** may need **-zinho** or just **-inho** to form a diminutive. You should learn the most common forms!

papel	+	inho	=	**papelinho**	small piece of paper
carrocel	+	zinho	=	**carrocelzinho**	small merry-go-round
barril	+	zito	=	**barrilzito**	small barrel

2.4.3.5   When **-inha, -inho, -ita, -ito** are added to nouns and adjectives ending in unstressed **-a, -e,** or **-o,** the final vowel is suppressed and the suffix is then added to the word:

fest(a)	+	inha	=	**festinha**	small party
gent(e)	+	inha	=	**gentinha**	people

grand(e)	+	inho	=	grandinho	biggish
quent(e)	+	inho	=	quentinho	warmish
tard(e)	+	inha	=	tardinha	early evening
cop(o)	+	ito	=	copito	a drink of wine
cop(o)	+	inho	=	copinho	small glass

But

pequeno > **pequenino** *or* **pequenininho**   very small/tiny

2.4.4 The most common augmentative suffixes are **-ão** for the masculine and **-ona** for the feminine. When they are added to the word, the final vowel of the root word is suppressed:

| livr(o) | + | ão | = | livrão | massive book |
| mes(a) | + | ona | = | mesona | huge table |

2.5 COMPOUND NOUNS

2.5.1 There are two ways of forming compound nouns in Portuguese.

2.5.1.1 Compounds can be formed by *juxtaposition* (the structure of the words is not modified):

pontapé	(ponta + pé)	a kick
terça-feira	(terça + feira)	Tuesday
cor-de-rosa	(cor + de + rosa)	pink

2.5.1.2 Compounds can also be formed by *agglutination* (the words contract and lose one or more of their phonetic elements):

| aguardente | (água + ardente) | brandy |

2.5.2 There are four different ways of forming the plural of compound nouns.

2.5.2.1 Both words take an **-s** if they are:

noun	+ noun	**couve-flor/couves-flores**	cauliflower
noun	+ adjective	**obra-prima/obras-primas**	masterpiece
adjective	+ noun	**má-língua/más-línguas**	gossiper
numeral	+ noun	**quinta-feira/quintas-feiras**	Thursday

2.5.2.2 The second word takes an **-s** if the two words are:

linked without hyphen	**passatempo/passatempos**	hobby
verb	+ noun	**guarda-chuva/guarda-chuvas**	umbrella
invariable	+ variable noun	**vice-rei/vice-reis**	viceroy

2.5.2.3   The first word takes an **-s** if the two words are:

linked by a preposition	**caminho-de-ferro/** **caminhos-de-ferro**	railway
second word defines first	**navio-escola/** **navios-escola**	training-ship

2.5.2.4   Both words stay the same in the plural if they are:

verb + adverb	**fala-barato**	wind-bag
verb + plural noun	**saca-rolhas**	corkscrew

2.6   COLLECTIVE NOUNS

Collective nouns are singular nouns that express the idea of a group of beings or things of the same kind:

uma alcateia	**(de lobos)**	pack
uma matilha	**(de cães)**	pack
um rebanho	**(de ovelhas)**	flock
uma manada	**(de bois/vacas)**	herd
um pomar	**(de árvores de fruto)**	orchard
um enxame	**(de abelhas)**	swarm
uma quadrilha	**(de ladrões)**	gang
um cardume	**(de peixes)**	school
uma multidão	**(de gente)**	crowd
uma cáfila	**(de camelos)**	caravan

3 ARTICLES

3.1 DEFINITE ARTICLE

o	(masc. sing.)	**o chão**	the floor
a	(fem. sing.)	**a porta**	the door
os	(masc. pl.)	**os tectos**	the ceilings
as	(fem. pl.)	**as janelas**	the windows

The definite article, which corresponds to 'the' in English, is used to designate a specific noun, with which it agrees in gender and number:

Ontem encontrei o Francisco, que lia o livro de francês.
Yesterday I met Francisco, who was reading his French book.

3.2 USE OF THE DEFINITE ARTICLE

3.2.1 With first names:[B] **O João, a Joana**.

Note: As a rule first names in Portuguese are preceded by a definite article (as opposed to Spanish, but similar to Catalan).

3.2.2 With titles:[B]

O senhor/a senhora/a menina quer uma chávena de chá?
Would you like a cup of tea?

A Sra. D. Laura Costa cozinha muito bem.[B]
Mrs Costa cooks very well.

A encomenda veio para o Sr. Dr. Gomes
The parcel is for Dr/Mr Gomes.

O Sr. Eng.º Costa não está. Quer deixar recado?
Mr Costa is not here. Would you like to leave a message?

(See terms of address below: 12.10.3 and 12.10.4.)

3.2.3 With names of continents, countries, islands and rivers:

a Europa	Europe	**a Madeira**	Madeira
o Brasil	Brazil	**o Tamisa**	the Thames
But	**(-) Portugal**	**(-) Angola**	
	(-) Cabo Verde	**(-) Moçambique**	

3.2.4   With days of the week:

A terça-feira é dia feriado.   *Tuesday is a bank holiday.*

3.2.5   Before possessive adjectives:[B]

a minha amiga   my friend   **o nosso carro**   our car

3.3   OMISSION OF THE DEFINITE ARTICLE

3.3.1   When referring to well-known or outstanding figures (except when a nuance of familiarity or disparagement is implied or when a reference to his/her work is made):

Gago Coutinho foi um aeronauta português.
Gago Coutinho was a Portuguese aeronaut.

But
O Gulbenkian tinha rios de dinheiro.
That Gulbenkian was rolling in it.

(a very free translation which conveys the flavour of the original)

3.3.2   When a title is used as a vocative:

Sente-se melhor agora, Sr. Gomes?
Are you feeling better now, Mr Gomes?

3.3.3   When a title includes a possessive pronoun:

Sua Majestade, o Rei de Espanha
His Majesty the King of Spain

Sua Excelência, o Presidente da República
His Excellency the President of the Republic

3.3.4   Usually before names of cities and towns:

Lisboa é a capital de Portugal.
Lisbon is the capital of Portugal.

Londres é a capital de Inglaterra.
London is the capital of England.

But
o Porto
o Rio de Janeiro

3.3.5 After the verbs **estudar**, **falar** and **tocar**:

Eu estudo química.	I study chemistry.
Eu falo espanhol.	I speak Spanish.
Eu toco piano.	I play the piano.

3.3.6 When making a generalization:

Eu adoro flores.   I love flowers.

But
Eu adoro as flores perfumadas.   I love fragrant flowers.

3.4 CONTRACTION OF THE DEFINITE ARTICLE

3.4.1 The definite article can be contracted with the prepositions **de**, **em**, **a** and **por** as follows.

3.4.1.1 Preposition **de** + article, meaning 'in', ''s', ', 'of', 'from':

de + o = do	**O melhor do mundo!** The best in the world!
de + a = da	**o livro da Manuela** Manuela's book
de + os = dos	**O teor dos discursos** ... The content of the speeches ...
de + as = das	**Ela é das Ilhas Gregas.** She is from the Greek Islands.

3.4.1.2 Preposition **em** + article, meaning 'on', 'at', 'about', 'of', 'in', 'into':

em + o = no	**O saco está no banco.** The bag is on the bench.
em + a = na	**Eu ando na universidade.** I am at university.
em + os = nos	**Ele pensa sempre nos filhos.** He always thinks of/about his children.
em + as = nas	**Já viste nas gavetas?** Have you checked in the drawers?

3.4.1.3   Preposition **a** + article, meaning 'on', 'to', 'at':

a + o = ao	**Ele está ao telefone.** He is on the phone.
a + a = à	**A minha avó vai à missa todos os domingos.** My grandmother goes to mass every Sunday.
a + os = aos	**Já enviámos as encomendas aos clientes.** We have already sent the parcels to our clients.
a + as = às	**O jantar de gala é às nove da noite.** The gala dinner is at 9 p.m.

3.4.1.4   Preposition **por** + article, meaning 'along', 'by', 'through', 'for':

por + o = pelo	**Siga pelo corredor da direita.** Go along the corridor on the right.
por + a = pela	**As informações foram dadas pela testemunha.** The information was provided by the witness.
por + os = pelos	**Nós corremos pelos campos.** We ran through the fields.
por + as = pelas	**Ela faz tudo pelas filhas.** She does everything for her daughters.

3.5   INDEFINITE ARTICLE

um	(masc. sing.)	**um jardim**	a garden
uma	(fem. sing.)	**uma escova**	a brush
uns	(masc. pl.)	**uns discos**	some/a few records
umas	(fem. pl.)	**umas praias**	some/a few beaches

The indefinite article, which corresponds to the English forms 'a', 'an' and 'some', is used to designate non-specific nouns, with which it agrees in gender and number.

> **Ontem encontrei um amigo num café.**
> Yesterday I met a friend in a café.

Note: Although **uns** and **umas** can be considered the plural of the indefinite article, the true plural of a *noun + indefinite article* in Portuguese is that noun in its plural form, standing alone. **Uns** and **umas** actually

convey the meaning of 'some' or **alguns/algumas**, as opposed to 'others',
outros/outras.

Havia uma flor em cima da mesa.
There was a flower on the table.

Havia flores em cima da mesa.
There were flowers on the table.

Havia umas flores em cima da mesa.
There were some flowers on the table.

3.6   USE OF THE INDEFINITE ARTICLE

3.6.1   To relate someone to a famous personality:

Ele não é propriamente um Camões, mas escreve poemas belíssimos.
He is not exactly a Camões, but he writes beautiful poems.

3.6.2   To indicate someone we do not know very well (could imply
disparaging tone):

Quem ganhou o concurso foi um Rui Sá.
The contest was won by a certain Rui Sá.

3.6.3   To indicate a piece of work by a famous person (usually a painter):

O André comprou um Vieira da Silva muito valioso.
André has bought a valuable Vieira da Silva.

Ele trazia um Armani.
He was wearing an Armani.

3.6.4   When it means 'a pair', 'about' or 'such':

umas calças e uns sapatos
a pair of trousers and a pair of shoes

Ficaram feridos uns quarenta homens.
About forty men were injured.

Tens umas ideias!
You have such (strange) ideas!

Ela tem uns lindos olhos!
She has such beautiful eyes!

3.7   OMISSION OF THE INDEFINITE ARTICLE

3.7.1   Before an unqualified noun, often indicating profession, rank or nationality:

O meu tio é dentista.   My uncle is a dentist.

But the article is used if the noun is qualified by an adjective, as a way of stressing the idea conveyed by that adjective:

O meu tio é um excelente dentista.
O meu tio é um dentista excelente.   My uncle is an excellent dentist.

3.7.2   When making a generalization:

O hotel estava cheio de belgas e alemães.
The hotel was full of Belgian and German guests.

3.8   CONTRACTION OF THE INDEFINITE ARTICLE

3.8.1   The indefinite article can be combined with the prepositions **em** and **de**.

3.8.1.1   Preposition **em** + indefinite article, meaning 'on a', 'in a', 'into such':

em + um = num	**Ele sentou-se num banco.** He sat on a bench.
em + uma = numa	**Ponha o bolo numa caixa, por favor.** Put the cake in a box, please.
em + uns = nuns	**O artigo usa-se nuns casos e omite-se noutros.** The article is used in some cases and omitted in others.
em + umas = numas	**Meti-me numas embrulhadas!** I got into such trouble!

3.8.1.2   Colloquial use of the preposition **de** + indefinite article, meaning 'of a', 'of some'. Although this use is possible, it should be avoided in educated written Portuguese.

de + um = dum	**o filho dum carpinteiro** the son of a carpenter
de + uma = duma	**a filha duma amiga** the daughter of a friend

de + uns = duns	**Preciso duns óculos.** I need some glasses.
de + umas = dumas	**A casa é dumas amigas.** The house belongs to some friends.

4 ADJECTIVES

4.1 GENDER

4.1.1 In matters of gender, adjectives tend to follow the same rules as nouns (see 2.1 and 2.2).

4.1.1.1 As a rule, adjectives have a feminine form in **-a** (especially adjectives in **-o**, **-ês**, **-or** and **-u**):

magro	**magra**	thin
inglês	**inglesa**	English (man/woman)
encantador	**encantadora**	charming
nu	**nua**	naked

But some adjectives ending in **-or** have the same form for both the masculine and the feminine:

anterior	anterior	**bicolor**	bicolour
posterior	posterior	**interior**	interior
incolor	colourless	**exterior**	exterior

And the same happens with the comparative form of adjectives:

maior	bigger	**inferior**	inferior
menor	smaller	**melhor**	better
superior	superior	**pior**	worse

4.1.1.2 Adjectives ending in **-eu** have a feminine form in **-eia**:

europeu	**europeia**	European
ateu	**ateia**	atheist

But

judeu	**judia**	Jewish

4.1.1.3 Adjectives ending in **-ão** can have feminine forms in **-ã**, **-oa** or **-ona**:

alemão	**alemã**	German
beirão	**beiroa**	native of Beira (Portugal)
brincalhão	**brincalhona**	playful

4.1.2 However, most adjectives ending in **-a**, **-e**, **-ar**, **-l**, **-m**, **-s** and **-z** in the masculine keep the same form in the feminine:

hipócrita	hypocritical	**original**	original
optimista	optimistic	**principal**	main
homicida	homicidal	**rural**	rural
agrícola	agricultural	**sensível**	sensitive
careca	bald	**terrível**	terrible
		possível	possible
doce	sweet	**cruel**	cruel
verde	green	**amável**	kind
forte	strong	**fácil**	easy
pobre	poor	**útil**	useful
triste	sad	**imbecil**	imbecile
grande	big	**difícil**	difficult
brilhante	brilliant	**gentil**	charming/kind
quente	hot	**azul**	blue
doente	ill		
prudente	prudent	**ruim**	bad/wicked
		comum	common
regular	regular	**jovem**	young
vulgar	ordinary		
		capaz	capable
simples	simple	**veloz**	fast
reles	vulgar	**feliz**	happy

But   **espanhol** (masc.) / **espanhola** (fem.)

4.1.3 Some adjectives have irregular feminine forms:

bom	**boa**	good
mau	**má**	bad

4.1.4 In compound adjectives only the second element takes the feminine form:

luso-britânico	**luso-britânica**	Luso–British

But

surdo-mudo	**surda-muda**	deaf–mute

4.2 NUMBER

4.2.1 In matters of number, adjectives tend to follow the same rules as nouns (see 2.3).

4.2.1.1   Adjectives ending in a vowel add an **-s** in the plural (see 2.3.1):

branco	brancos	white
branca	brancas	

4.2.1.2   Adjectives ending in a consonant (**-r, -s, -z**) add **-es** (see 2.3.2):

maior	maiores	bigger
francês	franceses	French
capaz	capazes	capable

4.2.1.3   Most adjectives ending in **-ão** change into **-ões**, a few into **-ães** and even fewer into **-ãos** (see 2.3.3):

espertalhão	espertalhões	cunning
alemão	alemães	German
são	sãos	healthy

4.2.1.4   Adjectives ending in **-m** change into **-ns** (see 2.3.4):

comum	comuns	common

4.2.1.5   Adjectives ending in **-al, -el, -ol** and **-ul** change into **-ais, -eis, -ois** and **-uis** (see 2.3.5):

leal	leais	loyal
cruel	crueis	cruel
espanhol	espanhois	Spanish
azul	azuis	blue

4.2.1.6   Adjectives ending in stressed **-il** form their plural by changing into **-is** (see 2.3.6):

imbecil	imbecis	imbecile

4.2.1.7   *But* adjectives ending in unstressed **-il** change into **-eis** in the plural (see 2.3.7):

útil	úteis	useful
versátil	versáteis	versatile

4.2.1.8   Adjectives ending in **-s** have the same form for both singular and plural (see 2.3.8):

uma canção simples / duas canções simples
one/two simple songs

um homem reles / dois homens reles
one/two vulgar men

4.2.2. In compound adjectives, only the second element takes the plural form:

luso-britânico   **luso-britânicos**   Luso–British

But

um rapaz surdo-mudo / dois rapazes surdos-mudos
one/two deaf–mute boys

4.3 DEGREE

4.3.1 The comparative

superiority	**mais ... (do) que**	more ... than
equality	**tão ... como**	as ... as
inferiority	**menos ... (do) que**	less ... than

Note: **Do que** is used to compare nouns, and **que** is used to compare adjectives:

A lebre é *mais* veloz *do que* a tartaruga.
The hare is fast*er than* the turtle.

O João é *mais* inteligente *que* estudioso.
João is *more* intelligent *than* studious.

O vinho é *tão* caro *como* a cerveja.
Wine is *as* expensive *as* beer.

O Outono é *menos* quente *do que* o Verão.
Autumn is *less* warm *than* Summer.

O João é *menos* estudioso *que* inteligente.
João is *less* studious *than* intelligent.

The adverbs **mais** and **menos** may be reinforced by **ainda** ('even'), **muito** ('much') or **bem** ('quite, far more'):

$$\text{O João é} \left\{ \begin{array}{l} \textbf{ainda} \\ \textbf{muito} \\ \textbf{bem} \end{array} \right\} \textbf{mais preguiçoso do que a Catarina.}$$

João is even/much/far more lazy than Catarina.

After the comparatives **anterior, posterior, inferior, superior** and **exterior**, the second term of the comparison is introduced by the preposition **a** (to):

O apartamento da Rua Direita é inferior a este.
The flat in Rua Direita is worse than this one.

A qualidade do *Expresso* é superior à de muitos jornais portugueses.[1]
The quality of the '*Expresso*' is superior to that of many Portuguese newspapers.

[1] Remember that preposition **a** + definite article **a** = **à** (see 3.4.1.3 above).

4.3.2 The superlative

4.3.2.1 Relative of superiority: **o, a, os, as mais . . . de/que**; of inferiority: **o, a, os, as menos . . . de/que**:

A Ana é *a* rapariga *mais* camarada *da* turma.
Ana is *the* friendl*iest* girl *in* the class.

O Jorge é *o* rapaz *menos* camarada *que* alguma vez conheci.
Jorge is *the least* friendly boy *that* I have ever met.

4.3.2.2 Absolute

4.3.2.2.1 The absolute superlative is usually formed by adding the suffix **-íssimo** to the adjective:

O Gustavo é engraçadíssimo. Gustavo is extremely funny.

Note: The ending of the adjective, however, may suffer some changes before the suffix **-íssimo** can be added:

(a) Adjectives ending in **-l**, **-r** and **-s** just add **-íssimo**:

original	**original*íssimo***	*extremely* original
vulgar	**vulgar*íssimo***	*extremely* ordinary
português	**português*íssimo***	*extremely* Portuguese

(b) In adjectives ending in a vowel the final vowel is suppressed before adding **-íssimo**:

calm(o)	**calm*íssimo***	*extremely* calm
trist(e)	**trist*íssimo***	*extremely* sad
baix(o)	**baix*íssimo***	*extremely* low/short

(c) Adjectives ending in **-vel** change into **-bilíssimo**:

agradá(vel)	**agrada*bilíssimo***	*most* pleasant
notá(vel)	**nota*bilíssimo***	*highly* notable
horrí(vel)	**horri*bilíssimo***	*utterly* horrible

(d) Adjectives ending in **-m** change into **-níssimo**:

comum   **comuníssimo**   *extremely* common

(e) Adjectives ending in **-z** change into **-císsimo**:

feliz   **felicíssimo**   *extremely* happy
veloz   **velocíssimo**   *extremely* fast

(f) Adjectives ending in **-ão** change into **-aníssimo**:

são   **saníssimo**   *extremely* healthy
temporão   **temporaníssimo**   *extremely* early (in the
                                                          season)

(g) Many adjectives revert to their Latin form before acquiring the
superlative endings **-íssimo**, **-ílimo** or **-érrimo**. You are advised to learn
this list by heart:

amigo	**amicíssimo**	*extremely* friendly
antigo	**antiquíssimo**	old
simples	**simplicíssimo**	simple
geral	**generalíssimo**	general
amargo	**amaríssimo**	bitter
doce	**dulcíssimo**	sweet
frio	**frigidíssimo**	cold
nobre	**nobilíssimo**	noble
sábio	**sapientíssimo**	wise/knowledgeable
difícil	**dificílimo**	difficult
fácil	**facílimo**	easy
pobre	**paupérrimo**	poor
célebre	**celebérrimo**	famous

4.3.2.2.2   The absolute superlative can also be formed by placing an
appropriate adverb before the adjective:

O Gustavo é *muito* engraçado.[1]   Gustavo is *very* funny.

Note: Although the regular form is advised in formal language, *in conversation, the superlative formed with adverbs is preferred:* **muito frio** instead
of **frigidíssimo**.

[1] **Muito** is the most commonly used adverb, but the following list can help to enrich your
use of Portuguese:

bastante	very	**extremamente**	extremely
excepcionalmente	exceptionally	**grandemente**	greatly
excessivamente	excessively	**imensamente**	immensely
extraordinariamente	extraordinarily	**terrivelmente**	terribly

4.3.3   Special comparative and superlative forms

	Comparative	*Superlative*	
		Relative	*Absolute*
bom	melhor[1]	o melhor	óptimo
mau	pior[2]	o pior	péssimo
grande	maior[3]	o maior	máximo
pequeno	menor[4]	o menor	mínimo
muito	mais	o mais	muitíssimo
pouco	menos	o menos	pouquíssimo
	superior	o superior	supremo
	inferior	o inferior	ínfimo

[1] Never **mais bom**.
[2] Never **mais mau**.
[3] Never **mais grande**.
[4] *But* **mais pequeno** is more frequently used than **menor**, although in Brazilian Portuguese **menor** is preferred.[B]

4.4   AGREEMENT

4.4.1   In Portuguese, adjectives always agree in gender and number with the nouns they qualify:

um senhor alt*o*	a tall gentleman
duas senhoras alt*as*	two tall ladies
a língua e a cultura portugues*a*	Portuguese language and culture
os casacos e os sapatos castanh*os*	the brown coats and the brown shoes

But if the nouns are of different gender, the adjective goes into the masculine plural:

as cadelas e os cães vadi*os*	the stray bitches and dogs
O livro e a caneta são nov*os*.	The book and the pen are new.

And if the nouns are of different number, the adjective changes to plural and agrees with the gender of the nouns it is qualifying:

os cães e o gato vadi*os*	the stray dogs and cat
a comida e as bebidas fri*as*	cold food and drinks
a revista e os livros frances*es*	the French magazine and books

4.5   POSITION IN THE SENTENCE

4.5.1   In Portuguese, adjectives usually follow the noun.

4.5.1.1   When the adjective describes a characteristic of the noun, such as colour, size, shape, taste, material, nationality or religion:

uma pasta azul	a blue briefcase
um tecido sedoso	a silky material
um livro grande	a large book
uma mulher holandesa	a Dutch woman
um saco redondo	a round bag
a religião católica	the Catholic religion
vinho doce	sweet wine

4.5.1.2   When the adjective is preceded by modifiers such as **muito**, **pouco**, **bastante**:

uma casa muito grande	a very big house

4.5.2   *But* the adjective can precede the noun in some cases.

4.5.2.1   If the relative superlative is used: **o melhor**, **o pior**, **o maior**, **o menor**:

O pior castigo é a prisão perpétua.
The worst punishment is life imprisonment.

4.5.2.2   With figurative meaning:

um grande homem	a great man
uma pobre mulher	an unfortunate woman
um velho amigo	a friend of many years

4.5.2.3   Sometimes we can place an adjective before the noun in order to use other adjectives after it, and thus avoid a long monotonous list of adjectives:

um aerodinâmico carro desportivo   an aerodynamic sports car

Note: When combining a series of adjectives, start with the more general and finish with the more particular:

Eles vivem num casarão enorme, velho, feio e frio.
They live in a huge, old, ugly, and cold mansion.

5 PRONOUNS

5.1 PERSONAL PRONOUNS

There are five types of personal pronouns in Portuguese:

- subject pronouns;
- direct object pronouns;
- indirect object pronouns;
- prepositional pronouns;
- reflexive pronouns.

5.1.1 Subject pronouns[B]

eu	I	**nós**	we
tu, você	you	**(vós), vocês**	you
ele, ela	he, she	**eles, elas**	they

Tu is only used when addressing friends, relatives and children. **Você** is a little more formal, but not formal enough to address either someone you have never met before or a superior, in which case you should use **o senhor** or **a senhora**.

Although **você** and **o senhor/a senhora** mean 'you' (2nd person sing.) in English, in Portuguese the verb must be in the third person singular. To help you understand why, imagine that you are actually saying 'You, Sir/Madam', but eventually you just say 'Sir/Madam' and drop the 'you' – grammatically you move on to a third person, but still mean 'you'!

Tu és muito simpático.
You (sing.) are very kind.

Você/o senhor/a senhora é muito simpático/a.
You (sing.) are very kind.

Vós is in parentheses in the above table because it is now considered an old-fashioned form of address, and is usually replaced by **vocês**. **Vocês** works as the plural of both **tu** and **você**. As above, although this form refers to the second person plural, the verb in Portuguese is in the third person plural:

Vós sois muito simpáticos.	You (pl.) are very kind.
Vocês são muito simpáticos.	You (pl.) are very kind.

5.1.1.1 Subject pronouns are usually omitted in Portuguese, because the verb already contains information on person and number:[B]

(tu) Vens ao cinema?   Are you coming to the cinema?
(nós) Estávamos à tua espera.   We were waiting for you.

5.1.1.2 *But* the subject pronoun must be specified whenever there is doubt as to whom the verb is referring:

Ele queria ir ao teatro.   He wanted to go to the theatre.
Eu queria ir ao cinema.   I wanted to go to the cinema.

5.1.1.3 The subject pronoun is also used to emphasize who is doing what:

Eu quero ir ao cinema, mas eles querem ir ao teatro.
I want to go to the cinema but they want to go to the theatre.

5.1.2   Direct object pronouns[B]

me	me	nos	us
te	you	vos	you
o, a	him, her, it	os, as	them

5.1.2.1 Usually the direct object pronoun follows the verb and is linked to it by a hyphen:[B]

(a) In affirmative statements:

Ele viu-*vos* à janela.   He saw *you* at the window.
Eu levo-*te* à estação.   I'll take *you* to the station.
Ela encontrou *o Rui*.   She met *Rui*.
Ela encontrou-*o*.   She met *him*.
O Rui viu *a Ana*. Ele viu-*a*.   Rui saw *Ana*. He saw *her*.

(b) In affirmative commands:

Come *o bolo*. Come-*o*.   Eat *the cake*. Eat *it*.

(c) In questions not introduced by an interrogative:

Viste-*o* ontem?   Did you see *him* yesterday?

(d) After co-ordinating conjunctions such as **e** ('and'), **mas** ('but'), **porém** ('however'), **todavia** ('nevertheless'), **contudo** ('however'):

Eu tinha duas canetas mas perdi-*as*.
I had two pens but I lost *them*.

Ele herdou uma fortuna, porém gastou-*a* em pouco tempo.
He inherited a fortune, however he lost *it* in a short time.

5.1.2.2 *But* the direct object pronoun precedes the verb in the following cases:

(a) In negative sentences (**não, nunca, jamais, nem, ninguém, nenhum**):

Ele não *nos* viu à janela.	He didn't see *us* at the window.
Nunca *o* tinha visto antes.	I had never seen *him* before.
Ninguém *o* soube.	Nobody knew *it*.

(b) In questions introduced by an interrogative (**quem?, qual?, quando?, onde?**, etc.):

Quem *me* faz um favor?	Who will do *me* a favour?
Onde *os* encontraste?	Where did *you* find them?

(c) After conjunctions such as **que** ('that') or **como** ('as'):

Acho que *me* viram à janela.
I think someone saw *me* at the window.

Como *os* queres preparar agora, aqui estaõ.
As/since/given that you want *them* prepared now, here they are.

(d) When it follows adverbs such as: **ainda, tudo, todos, sempre, também, talvez, pouco, bastante, muito**:

Ainda *os* tens?
Have you still got *them*?

Tudo *nos* recorda a nossa casa.
Everything reminds *us* of home.

Sempre *a* mudas para Leiria?
Are you finally moving *her* to Leiria?

Também *vos* lembram.
They also remember *you*.

Talvez *os* encontremos no cinema.
Perhaps *we* will meet them in the cinema.

Pouco *lhe* importa o que dizem.
He/she cares little for what they say.

Bastante *me* têm pedido que ignore o assunto.
I have been often asked to ignore the matter.

But the pronoun is placed *after* the verb if the adverb **sempre** is also placed after. Note that **sempre** is a modifier; it changes the meaning of the sentence depending on its position:

Eu encontro-*o* sempre na praia.
I always meet *him* at the beach.

Ontem sempre *o* encontrei no trabalho.
Yesterday I finally met *him* at work.

(e) When it follows adjectives or pronouns such as **todos/as, bastantes, muitos/muitas, poucos/as**:

Todas *me* lembram.
They all remember *me*.

Bastantes vezes *os* convidei.
I invited *them* many times.

Muitos são *os* chamados, mas poucos *os* escolhidos.
Many are called but few chosen.

5.1.2.3 In positive sentences with Future and Conditional Tenses the direct object pronoun is placed between the verb stem and ending, but in negative sentences it precedes the verbal form as usual:[B]

Essa decisão levá-lo-á à ruína.
That decision will lead you to ruin.

Mas esta alternativa não o levará à vitória.
But this alternative will not lead you to success.

Isso poder-me-ia afectar negativamente.
That could have a negative effect on me.

Mas não me importaria fazer nova tentativa.
But I would not mind having another go.

5.1.2.4 Variant forms of direct object pronouns:

(a) If the verb ends in a vowel or an oral diphthong, the pronoun is not altered:

A Maria fez um bolo e eu vi-*o*.
Maria baked a cake and I saw *it*.

Mas o João comeu-*o* todo sozinho.
But João ate *it* all by himself.

(b) If the verb ends in **-r**, **-s** or **-z**, these endings are omitted and the pronouns **-o**, **-a**, **-os**, **-as** change into **-lo**, **-la**, **-los**, **-las**:

Vamos partir o bolo. Vamos parti-*lo*.
Let's cut the cake. Let's cut *it*.

Perdemos a faca. Perdêmo-*la*.
We lost the knife. We lost *it*.

Diz a verdade. Di-*la*.
Tell the truth. Tell *it*.

But

Ele quer a faca. Ele quer*e-a*.
He wants the knife. He wants it.
Tu tens outra faca. Tu *tem-la*.
You have another knife. You have *it*.

Note: If the verb ends in **-ar** or **-az**, the **a** takes an acute accent:

Vou provar o bolo. Vou prov*á-lo*.
I'll try the cake. I'll try *it*.

A Maria faz bons bolos. Ela f*á-los*.
Maria bakes good cakes. She bakes *them*.

Note: If the verb ends in **-er** or **-ez**, the **e** takes a circumflex accent:

Vou comer o bolo. Vou com*ê-lo*.
I'll eat the cake. I'll eat *it*.

A Maria fez bolos. A Maria f*ê-los*.
Maria baked cakes. Maria baked *them*.

(c) If the verb ends in **-m**, **-ão**, **-õe** or **-ões**, the pronouns **-o**, **-a**, **-os**, **-as** change into **-no**, **-na**, **-nos**, **-nas**:

Eles sabem a verdade. Eles sabe*m-na*.
They know the truth. They know *it*.

Elas são corajosas. Elas s*ão-no*.
They are brave. They are *so*.

Elas põem a vida em risco. Ela p*õem-na* em risco.
They put their lives at risk. They put *them* at risk.

Note: What decides the pronominal forms **-no**, **-na**, **-nos**, **-nas** is the verbal ending in a nasal diphthong, even if spelt with **-em** or **-am**:

Elas contam as suas aventuras. Elas conta*m-nas*.
They tell their adventures. They tell *them*.

5.1.3   Indirect object pronouns[B]

me	me	**nos**	us
te	you	**vos**	you
lhe	him, her, it	**lhes**	them

5.1.3.1 As with the direct object pronoun, the indirect object pronoun
is linked to the verb by a hyphen and is placed after it in affirmative
sentences, commands, questions not introduced by an interrogative and
after co-ordinating conjunctions:

'Dê-*me* o dinheiro!', disse o ladrão.
'Give *me* the money!', said the thief.

Eu dei-*lhe* a carteira.
I gave *him* the handbag.

Deste-*lhe* mesmo? Sim, dei-*a*.
Did you really give it *to him*? Yes, I did (give *it*).

5.1.3.2 *But* it precedes the verb in negative and interrogative sentences,
and after certain adverbs, just as the direct object pronoun (see above,
5.1.2.2):

Não *lhes* digas que eu estive aqui.
Don't tell *them* I was here.

Quem *te* deu essa ideia?
Who gave *you* that idea?

Eles sempre *me* incomodam muito.
They always upset *me* deeply.

5.1.4 Contraction of the direct and indirect object pronouns

When direct and indirect object pronouns appear in the same sentence,
they can be contracted. The indirect object pronoun precedes the direct
object pronoun:

me + o	= *mo*	nos + o	= *no-lo*	(see 5.1.2.3)
me + a	= *ma*	nos + a	= *no-la*	
me + os	= *mos*	nos + os	= *no-los*	
me + as	= *mas*	nos + as	= *no-las*	
te + o	= *to*	vos + o	= *vo-lo*	
te + a	= *ta*	vos + a	= *vo-la*	
te + os	= *tos*	vos + os	= *vo-los*	
te + as	= *tas*	vos + as	= *vo-las*	
lhe + o	= *lho*	lhes + o	= *lho*	
lhe + a	= *lha*	lhes + a	= *lha*	
lhe + os	= *lhos*	lhes + os	= *lhos*	
lhe + as	= *lhas*	lhes + as	= *lhas*	

Ele deu-*me o livro.*	Ele deu-*mo.*	He gave *it to me.*
Ele deu-*te a revista.*	Ele deu-*ta.*	He gave *it to you.*
Ele deu-*lhe os sapatos.*	Ele deu-*lhos.*	He gave *them to him/her.*

Ele deu-*nos a caneta.*	Ele deu-*no-la.*	He gave *it to us.*
Ele deu-*vos os discos.*	Ele deu-*vo-los.*	He gave *them to you.*
Ele deu-*lhes a garrafa.*	Ele deu-*lha.*	He gave *it to them.*

Note: Word order is the same as for any direct or indirect object pronoun
(see 5.1.2.2):

| **Ela deu-te o livro?** | Did she give you the book? |
| **Não, ela não *mo* deu.** | No, she did not give *it to me.* |

5.1.5   Prepositional pronouns[B]

5.1.5.1 Prepositional pronouns are personal pronouns used with prepositions such as **de**, **em**, **para**, **por**, **sobre**:

mim	me	**nós**	us
ti, si[1]	you	**(vós)**, **vocês**[2]	you
ele, ela	him, she, it	**eles, elas**	them

Essas flores são *para mim*?
Are those flowers *for me*?

São. Foram enviadas *por eles*.
Yes. They were sent *by them*.

O que vai ser *de nós*?
What will become *of us*?

Não somos ninguém *sem ela*.
We are nothing *without her*.

Tenho um presente para *si/a senhora/o senhor/o sr. Dr.*, etc.[1]
I have a present for *you*.

Também há presentes para *vocês*.[2]
There are also presents for *you*.

[1] **Si** corresponds to the personal pronoun **você**. Sometimes, to avoid confusion, one can equally use the pronouns **o senhor**, **a senhora**, as objects of a preposition.

[2] The plural of **ti** and **si** is **vocês**, or **os senhores**, **as senhoras**, **Vs. Exas.**, etc. (since **vós** has become obsolete):

5.1.5.2 With the prepositions **com**, **em** and **de**, some prepositional pronouns change their form:

com + mim	=	comigo	com + nós	=	connosco
com + ti	=	contigo	com + vós	=	convosco
com + si	=	consigo			

But **com ele, com ela, com vocês, com eles, com elas**.

de + ele	=	dele	de + eles	=	deles
de + ela	=	dela	de + elas	=	delas

But **de mim, de ti, de nós, de vocês**.

em + ele	=	nele	em + eles	=	neles
em + ela	=	nela	em + elas	=	nelas

But **em mim, em ti, em nós, em vocês**.

Note: Prepositional pronouns preceded by the preposition **a** can be used emphatically after direct or indirect object pronouns:

Dá-me o livro *a mim*.
Give the book *to me* (not to someone else).

5.1.6   Reflexive pronouns[B]

eu lavo-*me*	I wash myself
tu lavas-*te*, você lava-*se*	you wash yourself
ele/ela lava-*se*	he/she washes himself/herself
nós lavamo-*nos*[1]	we wash ourselves
(vós lavai-*vos*), vocês lavam-*se*	you wash yourselves
eles/elas lavam-*se*	they wash themselves

[1]   When the pronoun is placed after a verbal form in the first person plural, the verb loses its final **-s** (**nós lavamos** – **nós lavamo-nos**).

5.1.6.1 As with direct and indirect object pronouns, the reflexive pronoun usually follows the verb (linked to it by a hyphen) except in negative and interrogative sentences, after conjunctions, prepositions and in relative clauses (see 5.1.2.2):

Ele sentou-*se*.	He sat down.
Mas ela não *se* sentou.	But she did not sit.
Elas choram porque *se* sentem tristes.	They cry because they feel sad.
Está na hora de *me* deitar.	It's time for me to go to bed.

Ele pediu-nos que *nos* levantássemos.	He asked us to stand up.
Quem *se* senta aqui?	Who is going to sit here?

5.1.6.2 The reflexive pronoun **se** – third person singular – is often used impersonally, translating the English 'you', 'one', 'they', 'people':

Neste restaurante come-*se* bem.	One can eat well in this restaurant.

5.2 POSSESSIVE PRONOUNS AND ADJECTIVES

Possessive pronouns and adjectives have exactly the same form in Portuguese, with the exception that the use of the article is optional with possessive pronouns.[B]

Possessive adjectives are placed between the definite article and the noun they qualify, whereas possessive pronouns replace the noun and may be preceded by the definite article to add emphasis or to denote a contrast:

Possessive adjective	*Possessive pronoun*
As *minhas* malas são pesadas.	**As malas pesadas são (*as*) *minhas*.**
My suitcases are heavy.	The heavy suitcases are *mine*.

5.2.1 Possessive adjectives[B]

o meu	a minha	os meus	as minhas	my
o teu/seu	a tua/sua	os teus/seus	as tuas/suas	your
o seu[1]	a sua	os seus	as suas	his/her
o nosso	a nossa	os nossos	as nossas	our
o vosso	a vossa	os vossos	as vossas	your
o seu[1]	a sua	os seus	as suas	their

[1] Since **seu/sua/seus/suas** can refer to the second person singular formal, to the third person singular and to the third person plural, some confusion often arises as to whom it refers. Therefore, **seu/sua/seus/suas** is usually replaced by a **de** phrase whenever it refers to the third persons:

o seu carro = o carro dele/dela/deles/delas
his/her/their car

a sua carteira = a carteira dele/dela/deles/delas
his/her/their wallet

O trabalho dela é mais completo do que o dele.
Her work is more thorough than his.

5.2.2   Possessive pronouns[B]

(o) **meu**	(a) **minha**	(os) **meus**	(as) **minhas**	mine
(o) **teu/seu**	(a) **tua/sua**	(os) **teus/seus**	(as) **tuas/suas**	yours
(o) **seu**[1]	(a) **sua**	(os) **seus**	(as) **suas**	his/hers
(o) **nosso**	(a) **nossa**	(os) **nossos**	(as) **nossas**	ours
(o) **vosso**	(a) **vossa**	(os) **vossos**	(as) **vossas**	yours
(o) **seu**[1]	(a) **sua**	(os) **seus**	(as) **suas**	theirs

[1]   These pronouns are usually replaced by a **de** phrase to avoid confusion (see 5.2.1).

5.2.3   In Portuguese, the ending of possessives agrees in gender and in number with the thing possessed and not with the possessor (as it does in English):

A Maria veio no *seu* **carro.**   Maria came in her car.
O Pedro veste a *sua* **camisa nova.**   Pedro puts on his new shirt.

5.2.4   As a rule, possessives are not used when the relationship between possessor and possessed is likely or obvious. This applies particularly to parts of the body, clothing or footwear; in this case, the definite article is preferred:

Ela veio no carro.
She came in her car.

A Ana falou com a mãe.
Ana spoke to her mother.

Abre a boca e fecha os olhos.
Open your mouth and close your eyes.

A Raquel vestiu a camisa.
Raquel put on her shirt.

Ele engraxou os sapatos.
He polished his shoes.

But if the possessor is not clear, the possessive must be used:

Os meus olhos são verdes.   My eyes are green.
A Ana visitou a minha mãe.   Ana visited my mother.

5.3   DEMONSTRATIVE PRONOUNS

este	**esta**	**estes**	**estas**	this/these (near the speaker)
esse	**essa**	**esses**	**essas**	that/those (near the hearer)
aquele	**aquela**	**aqueles**	**aquelas**	that/those (far from both)

Este é o meu amigo Henrique.
This is my friend Henrique.

Pode passar-me esse livro, por favor?
Can you pass me that book, please?

Aquele restaurante é muito bom.
That restaurant is very good.

5.3.1   In Portuguese, there are also neuter demonstrative pronouns. They are invariable and are used when the speaker cannot or will not identify an object precisely:

isto	this (near the speaker)
isso	that (near the hearer)
aquilo	that (far from both)

O que é isto?   What is this?
Isso é impossível!   That is impossible!
Aquilo deve ser um disco-voador.   That must be a flying saucer.

5.3.2   Demonstratives can be combined with the prepositions **de**, **em** and **a**:

de + este = deste	em + este = neste	
de + esta = desta	em + esta = nesta	
de + estes = destes	em + estes = nestes	
de + estas = destas	em + estas = nestas	
de + esse = desse	em + esse = nesse	
de + essa = dessa	em + essa = nessa	
de + esses = desses	em + esses = nesses	
de + essas = dessas	em + essas = nessas	

---

de + aquele = daquele	em + aquele = naquele
de + aquela = daquela	em + aquela = naquela
de + aqueles = daqueles	em + aqueles = naqueles
de + aquelas = daquelas	em + aquelas = naquelas
a + aquele = àquele	
a + aquela = àquela	
a + aqueles = àqueles	
a + aquelas = àquelas	

Não gosto deste vinho.	I don't like this wine.
O que é que tens nessas caixas?	What do you have in those boxes?
Nunca vi aquela peça.	I have never seen that play.

5.3.3 Neuter demonstrative pronouns also contract with the same prepositions as above:

de + isto = disto	em + isto = nisto
de + isso = disso	em + isso = nisso
de + aquilo = daquilo	em + aquilo = naquilo
a + aquilo = àquilo	

5.3.4 Agreement of demonstratives

Demonstratives used adjectivally agree in gender and number with the noun they precede. When qualifying more than one noun, they agree with the nearest:

este homem	this man
esta mulher	this woman
esses homens e mulheres	those men and women
aquelas mulheres e homens	those women and men

5.4 RELATIVE PRONOUNS

5.4.1

que	who, whom, which, that
o que, **a que**, **os que**, **as que**	the one that/who, the ones that/who, what

This is the most frequently used relative pronoun. It can refer to either people or things and may be used as the subject or object of a verb:

Aquela rapariga *que* falou contigo na festa é minha prima.
That girl *who* spoke to you at the party is my cousin.

O rapaz *que* vi esta manhã anda na minha turma.
The boy *whom* I saw this morning is in my class.

Esse livro é *o que* eu te comprei?
Is that book *the one* (*that*) I bought you?

Aquelas senhoras são *as que* me disseram para vir.
Those ladies are *the ones who* told me to come.

Isso foi *o que* ele disse!
That's *what* he said!

Note: In Portuguese, relative pronouns cannot be omitted as they sometimes can in English.

5.4.2

quem   who, whom, the one/the ones who

(a) **Quem** can be used instead of **que** when the verb **ser** introduces the subordinate clause (but **que** is also acceptable). In these cases, the pronoun **quem** takes the verb in the third person singular:

Foste tu *quem* contou o meu segredo!   It was you *who* revealed
Foste tu *que* contaste o meu segredo!   my secret!

(b) **Quem** is used when referring to a person and follows a preposition such as: **com**, **a**, **contra**, **entre**, **excepto**, **para**, **perante**, **por**, **salvo**, **segundo**, **sob**, **sobre**:

O rapaz com *quem* falei é de Lisboa.
The boy *whom* I talked to is from Lisbon.

Perante *quem* fizeste tal afirmação?
Before *whom* did you make such a statement?

Podem entrar todos, excepto *quem* não tem bilhete.
All welcome, except *those* without a ticket.

5.4.3

onde   where, in which

Refers to places:

Fui à casa *onde* viveu José Régio.
I went to the house *where* José Régio lived.

It may have some variations:

aonde   where   **donde**   from where, from which

A casa *aonde* vais pertenceu a José Régio.
The house you are going to belonged to José Régio.

A universidade *donde* vens é famosa.
The university *where* you are *from* is famous.

5.4.4

o qual, a qual, os quais, as quais   who, whom, which, that

Refers to people or things. It is preceded by a noun with which it agrees in gender and number (it can be used to replace the relative pronouns **que** and **quem**, in order to make the sentence clearer):

Os nossos vizinhos com *os quais* nos damos há anos, também vão.
Our neighbours, *whom* we have got on with for years, are also going.

Note: It is mainly used in written language; in colloquial Portuguese the sentence would be:

Os nossos vizinhos com *quem* nos damos há anos, também vão.

5.4.5

cujo, cuja, cujos, cujas   whose, of whom, of which

This pronoun implies ownership. It can also refer to people or things and is followed by a noun with which it agrees in gender and number:

Este é o homem *cujo* carro foi roubado.
This is the man *whose* car was stolen.

É esta a camisa *cujos* botões se perderam?
Is this the shirt the buttons *of which* have been lost?

5.4.6

quanto, quanta, quantos, quantas   all that/who, everything that, everyone who

This pronoun is normally preceded by the indefinite pronouns **tudo; todo, toda, todos, todas**:

Isto é tudo *quanto* sei.
This is *all* (*that*) I know.

Todos *quantos* **viram o acidente afirmaram ter sido por excesso de velocidade.**
All *who* saw the accident blamed it on excess speed.

5.5   INTERROGATIVE PRONOUNS

5.5.1

que, o que	what, which

Que queres?	What do you want?
O que queres?	
Que é uma bica?	What is a 'bica'?
O que é uma bica?	
Que cor preferes?	Which colour do you prefer?

5.5.2

quem	who
a quem	to whom
de quem	whose

Quem é aquele?	Who is that?
A quem ofereceste o colar?	To whom did you give the necklace?
De quem é aquele carro?	Whose car is that?

5.5.3

qual, quais	what, which (one)

Qual é o nome desta estação?	What is the name of this station?
Quais destas malas são as suas?	Which of these suitcases are yours?

Note: **Qual** expresses more clearly the idea of choice from a limited number of things than **que**. The main difference between these two interrogative pronouns is that **que** is usually followed by a noun but **qual** never is:

Que cor preferes?	What colour do you prefer?
Qual é a tua cor preferida?	Which is your favourite colour?

5.5.4

quanto, quanta, quantos, quantas	how much, how many

Quanto custa este vestido?	How much is this dress?
Quantas laranjas comeste?	How many oranges did you eat?

5.5.5   **É que** is often added to the interrogative pronouns to give emphasis:

O que *é que* **queres?**
Quem *é que* **é aquele?**
A quem *é que* **ofereceste o colar?**
De quem *é que* **é aquele carro?**
Qual *é que* **é a tua cor preferida?**
Quanto *é que* **custa este vestido?**

5.5.6   As well as these interrogative pronouns, some adverbs are also used to ask questions:

(a) **como** 'how':

Como está?	How are you?

(b) **onde** 'where':

Onde fica a casa-de-banho?	Where is the toilet?

(c) **porque, porquê** 'why':

Porque não vens? Porquê?	
Porque é que não vens?	Why aren't you coming? Why?

Note: Do not mistake it for **por que** (preposition **por** + pronoun):

Por que razão não vens?
For what reason (why) are you not coming?

Por que caminho seguiste?
Which route did you follow?

5.6   INDEFINITE PRONOUNS AND ADJECTIVES

algo	something
alguém	someone
certo, certa, certos, certas	certain
tal, tais	such
cada	each
vários, várias	various
bastante, bastantes	a lot
muito, muita, muitos, muitas	many
todo, toda, todos, todas	all, the whole of
tudo	everything
pouco, pouca, poucos, poucas	few
nenhum, nehuma, nenhuns, nenhumas	none
ninguém	no one
nada	nothing

Indefinite pronouns and adjectives refer to an undetermined third person or thing:

Há *algo* de errado com o carro.
There is *something* wrong with the car.

Não há *nada* de errado.
No, there is *nothing* wrong with it.

Alguém viu o Pedro?
Has *anyone* seen Pedro?

Não, *ninguém* o viu.
No, *no one* has seen him.

Perdi os meus livros. Viste *algum*?
I've lost my books. Have you seen *any* of them?

Não, não vi *nenhum*.
No, I haven*'t* seen *any*.

Tenho *muitos* amigos portugueses e *bastantes* amigos franceses, mas tenho *poucos* amigos russos.
I have *many* Portuguese friends and *quite a few* French friends but I have *few* Russian friends.

Certos carros são muito caros, mas não *todos*.[1]
Some cars are very expensive but not all.

Ele pensa que sabe *tudo*,[2] mas não sabe *nada*.
He thinks he knows *everything* but he knows *nothing*.

Ele adormece em *qualquer* lugar.
He falls asleep *anywhere*.

Estes bolos custam cem escudos *cada*, mas se comprares *vários* fica mais barato.
These cakes cost one hundred escudos *each* but if you buy *several* it's cheaper.

No *outro* dia fui ao teatro.
I went to the theatre the *other* day.

Foi uma *tal* Ana que me disse.
It was *someone* called Ana who told me.

Tais pessoas só gostam de boatos.
Such people only enjoy gossip.

[1] **Todo** agrees in gender and number with the noun it accompanies (**todo, toda, todos, todas**) and means 'all' in the sense of 'entire' or 'whole of'. It never precedes **isto, isso, aquilo**.

Comi o bolo todo.   I ate the whole cake.

[2] **Tudo** is invariable and means 'everything'. It is never used before a noun, but can precede **isto, isso, aquilo**.

Ele já sabia tudo isso.   He already knew all that.
Comi tudo o que estava na mesa.   I ate everything on the table.

6 NUMERALS

6.1 CARDINAL, ORDINAL AND MULTIPLICATIVE NUMBERS

	Cardinal	Ordinal	Multiplicative Augmentative[1]	Diminutive
0	zero			
1	um/uma	primeiro/a		
2	dois/duas	segundo/a	duplo/a, dobro	meio
3	três	terceiro/a	triplo/a	terço
4	quatro	quarto/a	quádruplo/a	quarto
5	cinco	quinto/a	quíntuplo/a	quinto
6	seis	sexto/a	sextuplo/a	sexto
7	sete	sétimo/a	septuplo/a	sétimo
8	oito	oitavo/a	octuplo/a	oitavo
9	nove	nono/a	nonuplo/a	nono
10	dez	décimo/a	décuplo/a	décimo
11	onze	décimo/a primeiro/a		onze avos
12	doze	décimo/a segundo/a		doze avos
13	treze	décimo/a terceiro/a		etc.
14	catorze[B]	décimo/a quarto/a		
15	quinze	décimo/a quinto/a		
16	dezasseis[B]	décimo/a sexto/a		
17	dezassete[B]	décimo/a sétimo/a		
18	dezoito	décimo/a oitavo/a		
19	dezanove[B]	décimo/a nono/a		
20	vinte	vigésimo/a		
21	vinte e um/uma	vigésimo/a primeiro/a		
22	vinte e dois/duas	vigésimo/a segundo/a		
23	vinte e três	vigésimo/a terceiro/a		
30	trinta	trigésimo/a		
40	quarenta	quadragésimo/a		
50	cinquenta	quinquagésimo/a		
60	sessenta	sexagésimo/a		
70	setenta	septuagésimo/a		
80	oitenta	octogésimo/a		
90	noventa	nonagésimo/a		
100	cem	centésimo/a	cêntuplo/a	

	Cardinal	*Ordinal*
101	cento e um/uma	centésimo/a primeiro/a
200	duzentos/as	ducentésimo/a
300	trezentos/as	tricentésimo/a
400	quatrocentos/as	quadringentésimo/a
500	quinhentos/as	quingentésimo/a
600	seiscentos/as	sexcentésimo/a
700	setecentos/as	septingentésimo/a
800	oitocentos/as	octingentésimo/a
900	novecentos/as	nongentésimo/a
1,000	mil	milésimo/a
1,000,000	um milhão	milionésimo/a
1,000,000,000	um bilhão um bilião	bilionésimo/a

[1] Often, instead of a multiplicative augmentative number, it is preferable to use the expression **vezes mais**:

Este valor é 25 vezes mais alto/baixo do que o anterior.
This amount is 25 times higher/lower than the previous one.

6.2   COLLECTIVE NUMERALS

um par 'a pair'	=	2
uma meia dúzia 'half a dozen'	=	6
uma dezena	=	10
uma dúzia 'dozen'	=	12
uma centena	=	100
um cento	=	100
uma grosa 'a gross'	=	144 (12 x 12)
um milhar	=	1,000

6.3   USE OF THE CONJUNCTION E WITH NUMERALS

35	trinta e cinco
349	trezentos *e* quarenta e nove
1,892	mil (–) oitocentos *e* noventa e dois
2,349	dois mil (–) trezentos *e* quarenta e nove

But

1,800	mil *e* oitocentos
1,700	mil *e* setecentos
2,100	dois mil *e* cem

Reading a long number is like making an enumeration where the last two elements are linked by the conjunction **e**. The **e** which is part of the tens group does not count.

Note: After 110,000, the number is read in groups of three figures:

293,272   duzentos *e* noventa *e* três mil (–)
                                              duzentos *e* setenta *e* dois

Note: Where numbers have been given in figures in this chapter they have
been written in the English style. In Portuguese, however, the decimal
point is replaced by a decimal comma. A point is used to separate the
thousands:

Portuguese	*English*
2,5 kg = 2.500 g	2.5 kg = 2,500 g
35,6 km = 35.600 m	35.6 km = 35,600 m

6.4 ROMAN NUMERALS

Roman numerals are used in Portuguese to refer to centuries and in
monarchs' and popes' names. When reading them, use an ordinal up to
and including IX and a cardinal from X onwards.

**D. João I (primeiro) foi o fundador da segunda dinastia em finais do
séc. XIV (século catorze).**
King João I was the founder of the second Portuguese dynasty at the
end of the fourteenth century.

João XXI (vinte e um) foi um papa português.
John XXI was a Portuguese pope.

No século VIII (oitavo) os Árabes invadiram a Península Ibérica.
The Arabs invaded the Iberian Peninsula in the eighth century.

7 VERBS[B]

7.1 MOODS AND TENSES

The following shows all possible moods and tenses of the first person singular of the regular **-ar** verb **estudar**. It is intended for reference only; the following pages give full conjugations for all tenses.

Indicative mood

Present tenses	Present	**estudo**
	Present Perfect	**tenho estudado**
Past tenses	Imperfect	**estudava**
	Preterite	**estudei**
	Past Perfect	**tinha estudado**
	Pluperfect	**estudara**
Future tenses	Future	**estudarei**
	Future Perfect	**terei estudado**
	Conditional	**estudaria**
	Conditional Perfect	**teria estudado**

Subjunctive mood

Present tenses	Present	**estude**
	Present Perfect	**tenha estudado**
Past tenses	Past	**estudasse**
	Past Perfect	**tivesse estudado**
Future tenses	Future	**estudar**
	Future Perfect	**tiver estudado**

Imperative mood	**estuda (tu)**
	estude (você)
	estudemos (nós)
	estudai (vós)
	estudem (vocês)

Infinitive	**estudar**
Compound Infinitive	**ter estudado**
Present Participle (gerund)	**estudando**
Compound Present Participle	**tendo estudado**
Past Participle	**estudado**

In Portuguese there are four main groups of verbs:

(a) 1st conjugation: all verbs with Infinitives ending in **-ar**;
(b) 2nd conjugation: all verbs with Infinitives ending in **-er**;
(c) 3rd conjugation: all verbs with Infinitives ending in **-ir**;
(d) 4th conjugation: all derivatives of the verb **pôr**.

To form the simple tenses of regular verbs, remove the ending of the Infinitive (**-ar**, **-er**, **-ir**, **-or**). Add the endings shown below to the stem of the verb, for example:

estud*ar* = **estud*o*** (first person singular of the Present Indicative)

The compound tenses of regular verbs are formed by the auxiliary verb **ter** (in the appropriate person) + Past Participle of the main verb, for example:

ter estudado = *tenho* **estudado** (first person singular of the Present Perfect Indicative)

7.2   INDICATIVE MOOD

7.2.1   Present

7.2.1.1   Meanings

(a) Action in the present:

Que *fazes*?	What *are you doing*?
***Leio* o jornal.**	*I am reading* the paper.

(b) Habitual or repetitive action in the present:

Ela *viaja* muito.
She *travels* a lot.

Eu *chego* sempre às nove da manhã.
I always *arrive* at 9 a.m.

(c) Universal statement:

Dois mais dois *são* quatro.
Two and two *are* four.

O sol quando *nasce* é para todos.
When the sun *rises* it is for everyone.

(d) Replacing the Future tense:

Eu *vou* ao cinema amanhã.
I *am going* to the cinema tomorrow.

(e) Historical Present:

Em 1500 Pedro Álvares Cabral *descobre* o Brasil.
In 1500 Pedro Álvares Cabral *discovers* Brazil.

7.2.1.2   Conjugation

	cant*ar* 'to sing'	**vend*er*** 'to sell'	**part*ir*** 'to leave'	**pôr** 'to put'
eu	cant*o*	vend*o*	part*o*	po*nho*
tu	cant*as*	vend*es*	part*es*	põ*es*
ele,ela,você	cant*a*	vend*e*	part*e*	põ*e*
nós	cant*amos*	vend*emos*	part*imos*	po*mos*
(vós)	cant*ais*	vend*eis*	part*is*	po*ndes*
eles, elas, vocês	cant*am*	vend*em*	part*em*	põ*em*

Note: If the stem vowel in **-ir** verbs is an **e** or an **o**, it becomes **i** or **u** respectively in the first person singular:

e to i		*o to u*	
d*e*spir	eu d*i*spo	c*o*brir	eu c*u*bro
m*e*ntir	eu m*i*nto	d*o*rmir	eu d*u*rmo
pref*e*rir	eu pref*i*ro	t*o*ssir	eu t*u*sso
rep*e*tir	eu rep*i*to		
s*e*guir	eu s*i*go		
s*e*rvir	eu s*i*rvo		
v*e*stir	eu v*i*sto		

Note: If the stem of the **-ar** verb ends in **-c**, **-ç** or **-g**, these consonants change into **-qu**, **-c** or **-gu** respectively when they are followed by an **-e**, in order to preserve the original consonant sound of the stem:

fi*c*ar	eu fi*qu*ei
co*ç*ar	eu co*c*ei
che*g*ar	eu che*gu*ei

Note: If the stem of an **-er** or **-ir** verb ends in **-c** or **-gu**, these consonants change into **-ç** and **-j** or **-g** respectively when they are followed by an **-o** or an **-a**, also to preserve the original consonant sound of the stem:

ven*c*er	eu ven*ç*o
fu*g*ir	eu fu*j*o
er*gu*er	eu er*g*o

7.2.1.3   Irregular Present

ser	sou, és, é, somos, sois, são
estar	estou, estás, está, estamos, estais, estão
ter	tenho, tens, tem, temos, tendes, têm
haver[1]	há
dar	dou, dás, dá, damos, dais, dão
ir	vou, vais, vai, vamos, ides, vão
vir	venho, vens, vem, vimos, vindes, vêm
ver	vejo, vês, vê, vemos, vedes, vêem
dizer	digo, dizes, diz, dizemos, dizeis, dizem
fazer	faço, fazes, faz, fazemos, fazeis, fazem
trazer	trago, trazes, traz, trazemos, trazeis, trazem
ouvir	ouço, ouves, ouve, ouvimos, ouvis, ouvem
pedir	peço, pedes, pede, pedimos, pedis, pedem
medir	meço, medes, mede, medimos, medis, medem
saber	sei, sabes, sabe, sabemos, sabeis, sabem

[1] **Haver** can only be used in the third person singular:

Há muitas crianças pobres.   *There are* many poor children.

Haver-de, however, can be used as an auxiliary verb expressing the intention of doing something in the future:

Hei-de ler o livro que me recomendaste.   I shall read the book you recommended.

7.2.2   Present Perfect

7.2.2.1   Meanings

Note that this tense is called 'Present Perfect' and not 'Perfect' in Portuguese. Whereas in English this tense is more of an aspect or refers to a state of completion following an action, in Portuguese it has the function of a progressive tense describing an action or a process going on over some length of time.

(a) Action which started in the past and has been developing over a period of time, and which may or may not continue into the future:

Eu *tenho estudado* muito.   I *have been studying* very hard.

(b) Continuity:

Ultimamente *tenho-me interessado* pela política internacional.
Lately *I have been interested* in international politics.

(c) Repetition:

Eu *tenho ido* ao teatro.   I *have been going* to the theatre.

But the only exception is **tenho dito**, a formula used for closing a speech which therefore does express a fully completed action in the past.

7.2.2.2   Conjugation (Present of **ter** + past participle of the verb)

		cantar	**vend**er	**part**ir	**pôr**
eu	*tenho*				
tu	*tens*				
ele, ela, você	*tem*	cantado	vendido	partido	posto
nós	*temos*				
(vós)	*tendes*				
eles, elas, vocês	*têm*				

7.2.3   Imperfect

7.2.3.1   Meanings

(a) Past action of a certain duration:

Quando a minha avó *era* nova não havia televisão.
When my grandmother *was* young there was no television.

(b) Frequency or habit:

Todas as manhãs eu *ia* de autocarro para a escola.
Every morning I *went* to school by bus.

(c) Two simultaneous actions:

Enquanto ele *lia* o jornal, ela *preparava* o jantar.
While he *read* the paper, she *made* the dinner.

(d) When describing background action and an incident, the background action is always expressed in the Imperfect:

Eu *dormia* quando tu chegaste.   I *was sleeping* when you arrived.

Note: The progressive form **estar a** + infinitive can also describe a background action in the past:

Eu *estava a dormir* quando tu chegaste.
I *was sleeping* when you arrived.

instead of

Eu *dormia* quando tu chegaste.

(e) Polite request (in the sense of 'would' or 'could'):

Podia-me dizer as horas, por favor?
Could you please tell me the time?

(f) Replacing the Conditional tense:

Se eu tivesse muito dinheiro, *comprava* um iate.
If I had a lot of money, *I would buy* a yacht.

7.2.3.2   Conjugation

	cantar	**vender**	**partir**	**pôr**
eu	cantava	vendia	partia	punha
tu	cantavas	vendias	partias	punhas
ele, ela, você	cantava	vendia	partia	punha
nós	cantávamos	vendíamos	partíamos	púnhamos
(vós)	cantáveis	vendíeis	partíeis	púnheis
eles, elas, vocês	cantavam	vendiam	partiam	punham

7.2.3.3   Irregular Imperfect

ser	era, eras, era, éramos, éreis, eram
ter	tinha, tinhas, tinha, tínhamos, tínheis, tinham
vir	vinha, vinhas, vinha, vínhamos, vínheis, vinham

7.2.4   Preterite

7.2.4.1   Meanings

(a) Completed action in the past:

Eu *estudei* português no ano passado.
I *studied* Portuguese last year.

(b) When describing background action and an incident, the Preterite is always used to express the incident:

Eu dormia quando tu *chegaste*.
I was sleeping when you *arrived*.

7.2.4.2   Conjugation

	cant**ar**	vend**er**	part**ir**	p**ôr**
eu	cant*ei*	vend*i*	part*i*	p*us*
tu	cant*aste*	vend*este*	part*iste*	pus*este*
ele, ela, você	cant*ou*	vend*eu*	part*iu*	p*ôs*
nós	cant*ámos*	vend*emos*	part*imos*	pus*emos*
(vós)	cant*astes*	vend*estes*	part*istes*	pus*estes*
eles, elas, vocês	cant*aram*	vend*eram*	part*iram*	pus*eram*

7.2.4.3   Irregular Preterite

ser	fui, foste, foi, fomos, fostes, foram
estar	estive, estiveste, esteve, estivemos, estivestes, estiveram
ter	tive, tiveste, teve, tivemos, tivestes, tiveram
haver	houve
dar	dei, deste, deu, demos, destes, deram
ir	fui, foste, foi, fomos, fostes, foram
vir	vim, vieste, veio, viemos, viestes, vieram
ver	vi, viste, viu, vimos, vistes, viram
dizer	disse, disseste, disse, dissemos, dissestes, disseram
fazer	fiz, fizeste, fez, fizemos, fizestes, fizeram
querer	quis, quiseste, quis, quisemos, quisestes, quiseram
saber	soube, soubeste, soube, soubemos, soubestes, souberam
trazer	trouxe, trouxeste, trouxe, trouxemos, trouxestes, trouxeram

7.2.4.4   Differences between the Preterite and the Present Perfect

In English we can use either the Simple Past or the Present Perfect to express a completed action in the past:

Yesterday I *studied* hard.
I have *studied* hard.

In Portuguese, only the *Preterite* expresses a fully completed action in the past. The *Present Perfect* expresses an action which began in the past, has been developing over a period of time and may or may not continue into the future (see 7.2.2.1):

Eu *encontrei* a Teresa na biblioteca.
I *met* Teresa in the library.

Eu *tenho encontrado* a Teresa na biblioteca.
I *have been meeting* Teresa in the library (and I may still continue meeting her in the library).

7.2.4.5 Differences between Preterite and Imperfect

(a) The *Preterite* expresses a past action limited by time while the Imperfect expresses a past action with a certain duration and not limited in time:

Ontem a Carla *levantou-se* às oito horas.
Yesterday Carla *got up* at eight o'clock.

Dantes a Carla *levantava-se* às oito horas.
Carla *used to get up* at eight o'clock.

(b) The *Preterite* is used to express a single event, while the Imperfect expresses an habitual action:

Quando *vi* o teu pai, *perguntei-lhe* por ti.
When I *saw* your father I *asked* (*him*) about you.

Quando *via* o teu pai, *perguntava-lhe* por ti.
Whenever I *saw* your father I *would ask* (*him*) about you.

7.2.5 Past Perfect and Pluperfect

7.2.5.1 Meanings

(a) Past action prior to another action in the past:

Eu *tinha saído* quando ela chegou.
I *had left* when she arrived.

Note: The Pluperfect is almost exclusively used in literary language. In colloquial Portuguese, the Past Perfect is used instead:

O livro *tinha-se tornado* tão maçador que adormeci.
The book *had become* so boring that I fell asleep.

instead of

O livro *tornara-se* tão maçador que adormeci.

7.2.5.2 Conjugation

		cantar	*vender*	*partir*	*pôr*
Past Perfect					
eu	*tinha*				
tu	*tinhas*				
ele, ela, você	*tinha*	cantado	vendido	partido	posto
nós	*tínhamos*				
(vós)	*tínheis*				
eles, elas, vocês	*tinham*				

	cant*ar*	**vend*er***	**part*ir***	**pô*r***
Pluperfect				
eu	cant*ara*	vend*era*	part*ira*	pus*era*
tu	cant*aras*	vend*eras*	part*iras*	pus*eras*
ele, ela, você	cant*ara*	vend*era*	part*ira*	pus*era*
nós	cant*áramos*	vend*êramos*	part*íramos*	pus*éramos*
(vós)	cant*áreis*	vend*êreis*	part*íreis*	pus*éreis*
eles, elas, vocês	cant*aram*	vend*eram*	part*iram*	pus*eram*

7.2.5.3   Irregular pluperfect

ser   fora, foras, fora, fôramos, fôreis, foram
dar   dera, deras, dera, déramos, déreis, deram
ir   fora, foras, fora, fôramos, fôreis, foram
vir   viera, vieras, viera, viéramos, viéreis, vieram
fazer   fizera, fizeras, fizera, fizéramos, fizéreis, fizeram

7.2.6   Future

7.2.6.1   Meanings

(a) Future action, either definite or most probable:

Amanhã *telefonarei* à Isabel.
I will phone Isabel tomorrow.

(b) Uncertainty about present facts:

Será que está a chover?
Do you think it is raining?

Bateram à porta. Será o Filipe?
Someone has knocked at the door. *Do you think* it is Filipe?

(c) Condition (probability):

Se estudares, *passarás*.
If you study, *you will pass*.

Note: The Future is usually reserved for formal language, especially rules, regulations and legislation. In colloquial Portuguese it is replaced by the Present or the Present of **ir** + infinitive of the verb:

Amanhã *telefono* à Isabel.
I'll phone Isabel tomorrow.

Amanhã *vou telefonar* à Isabel.
I'm going to phone Isabel tomorrow.

instead of

Amanhã *telefonarei* **à Isabel.**

7.2.6.2 Conjugation

	cantar	**vender**	**partir**	**pôr**
eu	cantar*ei*	vender*ei*	partir*ei*	por*ei*
tu	cantar*ás*	vender*ás*	partir*ás*	por*ás*
ele, ela, você	cantar*á*	vender*á*	partir*á*	por*á*
nós	cantar*emos*	vender*emos*	partir*emos*	por*emos*
(vós)	cantar*eis*	vender*eis*	partir*eis*	por*eis*
eles, elas, vocês	cantar*ão*	vender*ão*	partir*ão*	por*ão*

7.2.6.3 Irregular Future

dizer	direi, dirás, dirá, diremos, direis, dirão
fazer	farei, farás, fará, faremos, fareis, farão
trazer	trarei, trarás, trará, traremos, trareis, trarão

7.2.7 Future Perfect

7.2.7.1 Meanings

(a) Future action prior to another action in the future:

Quando eles chegarem, já nós *teremos almoçado.*
When they arrive, we *will have had* our lunch.

(b) Uncertainty about past facts:

Já *terá passado* **a chuva?**   *Will it have stopped* raining?
Quem *terá partido* **este copo?**   Who *might have broken* this glass?

7.2.7.2 Conjugation

		cantar	**vender**	**partir**	**pôr**
eu	*terei*				
tu	*terás*				
ele, ela, você	*terá*	cantado	vendido	partido	posto
nós	*teremos*				
(vós)	*tereis*				
eles, elas, vocês	*terão*				

7.2.8   Conditional

7.2.8.1   Meanings

(a) Uncertainty about past facts:

Quem *seria* aquele homem de fato escuro?
Who *could* that man in the dark suit *be*?

(b) Polite request implying wishing:

***Gostaria* que me desse a sua opinião sobre este assunto.**
I would like you to give me your opinion on this matter.

(c) Condition of a fact that probably will not happen:

Se eu tivesse tempo, *iria* à praia.
If I had the time, *I would go* to the beach.

Note: The Conditional is usually replaced by the Imperfect:

Se eu tivesse tempo, *ia* à praia.
If I had the time, *I would go* to the beach.

instead of

Se eu tivesse tempo, *iria* à praia.

7.2.8.2   Conjugation

	cant*ar*	vend*er*	part*ir*	p*ôr*
eu	cantar*ia*	vender*ia*	partir*ia*	por*ia*
tu	cantar*ias*	vender*ias*	partir*ias*	por*ias*
ele, ela, você	cantar*ia*	vender*ia*	partir*ia*	por*ia*
nós	cantar*íamos*	vender*íamos*	partir*íamos*	por*íamos*
(vós)	cantar*íeis*	vender*íeis*	partir*íeis*	por*íeis*
eles, elas, vocês	cantar*iam*	vender*iam*	partir*iam*	por*iam*

7.2.8.3   Irregular Conditional

dizer	diria, dirias, diria, diríamos, diríeis, diriam
fazer	faria, farias, faria, faríamos, faríeis, fariam
trazer	traria, trarias, traria, traríamos, traríeis, trariam

7.2.9   Conditional Perfect

7.2.9.1   Meanings

(a) Condition of a past action which did not happen:

Eu *teria tido* uma boa nota se tivesse estudado.
I *would have had* a good mark if I had studied.

(b) Uncertainty about past facts:

Quem *teria partido* este copo?   Who *could have broken* this glass?

7.2.9.2.   Conjugation

		cantar	vender	partir	pôr
eu	teria				
tu	terias				
ele, ela, você	teria	cantado	vendido	partido	posto
nós	teríamos				
(vós)	teríeis				
eles, elas, vocês	teriam				

Note: If any object pronouns are used with the Future or Conditional they are placed between the stem and the ending of the verb and linked by hyphens:

Ela escrever-*me*-á uma carta.   She will write *me* a letter.
Ela escrevê-*la*-ia a mim.   She would write *it* to me.

(See 5.1.2.1 for word order and also 5.1.2.4 for variant forms of direct object pronouns.)

7.3   SUBJUNCTIVE MOOD

The *Indicative mood* expresses real facts whereas the *Subjunctive mood* expresses facts which are uncertain, doubtful, eventual or even unreal:

Hoje vamos fazer um piquenique, por isso espero que não *chova*.
Today we are going for a picnic, so I hope it does not *rain*.

The *Subjunctive* is linked to the idea of command, wishing, feeling, doubt and necessity, and normally appears in subordinate clauses. It is used after the following verbs and expressions:

(a) Indirect command:

querer que   pedir que   ordenar que

(b) Wishing or feeling:

querer que	lamentar que	ser bom que/se
pedir que	oxalá	tomara que
esperar que	ser pena que/se	Deus queira que

(c) Doubt or uncertainty:

duvidar que	pode ser que	talvez
ser provável/improvável que	não achar que	se
ser possível/impossível que	não parecer que	caso

(d) Necessity:

ser preciso que	ser necessário que	ser importante que

(e) Other conjunctions and adverbs:

embora	por muito que	logo que
mesmo que	por pouco que	enquanto
ainda que	quem quer que	quando
para que	onde quer que	sempre que
por mais que	o que quer que	como se
por menos que	assim que	

7.3.1　Present Subjunctive

7.3.1.1　Meanings

(a) Actions referring to a present situation:

É pena que ela *esteja* doente.　　It is a pity that she *is* ill.

(b) Actions referring to a future situation:

Quando eu voltar, é bom que o teu quarto *esteja* arrumado!
When I get back, you'd better have your room tidy!

7.3.1.2　Conjugation

	cant*ar*	**vend*er***	**part*ir***	**p*ôr***
eu	cant*e*	vend*a*	part*a*	ponh*a*
tu	cant*es*	vend*as*	part*as*	ponh*as*
ele, ela, você	cant*e*	vend*a*	part*a*	ponh*a*
nós	cant*emos*	vend*amos*	part*amos*	ponh*amos*
(vós)	cant*eis*	vend*ais*	part*ais*	ponh*ais*
eles, elas, vocês	cant*em*	vend*am*	part*am*	ponh*am*

7.3.1.3   Irregular Present Subjunctive

ser	seja, sejas, seja, sejamos, sejais, sejam
estar	esteja, estejas, esteja, estejamos, estejais, estejam
haver	haja
dar	dê, dês, dê, demos, deis, dêem
ir	vá, vás, vá, vamos, vades, vão
querer	queira, queira, queira, queiramos, queirais, queiram
saber	saiba, saibas, saiba, saibamos, saibais, saibam

7.3.2   Present Perfect Subjunctive

7.3.2.1   Meanings

(a) Actions referring to a past situation:

Espero que *tenham feito* uma boa viagem.
I hope *you have had* a good trip.

(b) Actions referring to a future situation:

É provável que às cinco horas *tenhas acabado* o exame.
You probably *will have finished* your exam by five o'clock.

7.3.2.2   Conjugation

		cant*ar*	**vend*er***	**part*ir***	**pôr**
eu	*tenha*				
tu	*tenhas*				
ele, ela, você	*tenha*	cantado	vendido	partido	posto
nós	*tenhamos*				
(vós)	*tenhais*				
eles, elas, vocês	*tenham*				

7.3.3   Past Subjunctive

7.3.3.1   Meanings

The Past Subjunctive is always used in subordinate clauses. The verb in the main clause can be in the Imperfect or in the Preterite, and their respective use changes the meaning of the sentence:

(a) The Imperfect is used for actions referring to a present or future situation:

Eu *queria* que *viesses* almoçar comigo hoje ou amanhã.
I *would like* you to have lunch with me today or tomorrow.

(b) The Preterite is used for actions referring to a past situation:

Eu *quis* que *viesses* almoçar comigo ontem (mas tu não vieste).
I *wanted* you to have lunch with me yesterday (but you did not come).

(c) The Past Subjunctive is also used to express a condition to a fact that probably will not happen. It can be used with the Conditional or the Imperfect:

Se eu *tivesse* dinheiro compraria/comprava um barco.
If I *had* money I would buy a boat.

7.3.3.2   Conjugation

	cant*ar*	**vend*er***	**part*ir***	**p*ôr***
eu	cant*asse*	vend*esse*	part*isse*	pus*esse*
tu	cant*asses*	vend*esses*	part*isses*	pus*esses*
ele, ela, você	cant*asse*	vend*esse*	part*isse*	pus*esse*
nós	cant*ássemos*	vend*êssemos*	part*íssemos*	pus*éssemos*
(vós)	cant*ásseis*	vend*êsseis*	part*ísseis*	pus*ésseis*
eles, elas, vocês	cant*assem*	vend*essem*	part*issem*	pus*essem*

7.3.4   Past Perfect Subjunctive

7.3.4.1   Meanings

(a) Past action prior to another past action:

Não acreditei que ele *tivesse dito* a verdade.
I did not believe he *had told* the truth.

(b) Past condition to a past fact that did not happen:

Se *tivesse tido* muito dinheiro, teria comprado um avião.
If *I had had* a lot of money, I would have bought a plane.

7.3.4.2   Conjugation

		cant*ar*	**vend*er***	**part*ir***	**p*ôr***
eu	*tivesse*				
tu	*tivesses*				
ele, ela, você	*tivesse*				
nós	*tivéssemos*	cantado	vendido	partido	posto
(vós)	*tivésseis*				
eles, elas, vocês	*tivessem*				

7.3.5 Future Subjunctive

7.3.5.1 Meanings

Eventuality of a future action:

Vem-me ajudar, se *puderes*.   Help me, if *you can*.

The Future Subjunctive is used after words referring to a future or uncertain action: **se**, **quando**, **enquanto**, **logo que**, **assim que**, **como**:

se quiseres	if you wish
quando quiseres	when you wish
enquanto quiseres	as long as you wish
logo que/assim que quiseres	as soon as you wish
como quiseres	as you wish

Note: In Portuguese, the translation of the English 'whatever', 'whoever', 'whenever' and 'wherever' is followed by the Future Subjunctive:

Podes fazer o que *quiseres*.   You can do whatever *you wish*.

7.3.5.2 Conjugation

	cant*ar*	**vend*er***	**part*ir***	**pôr**
eu	cant*ar*	vend*er*	part*ir*	pus*er*
tu	cant*ares*	vend*eres*	part*ires*	pus*eres*
ele, ela, você	cant*ar*	vend*er*	part*ir*	pus*er*
nós	cant*armos*	vend*ermos*	part*irmos*	pus*ermos*
(vós)	cant*ardes*	vend*erdes*	part*irdes*	pus*erdes*
eles, elas, vocês	cant*arem*	vend*erem*	part*irem*	pus*erem*

7.3.6 Future Perfect Subjunctive

7.3.6.1 Meaning

Future action prior to another action also in the future. The Future Subjunctive follows the words **se**, **quando**, **logo que** and **assim que**:

Se *tiveres terminado* quando eu chegar, vamos juntos ao cinema.
If *you have finished* by the time I arrive, we will go to the cinema together.

Quando *tiver acabado* o curso vou para Itália.
When *I have finished* my degree I will go to Italy.

Logo que/assim que *tiver vendido* o carro antigo compro um novo.
As soon as *I have sold* my old car I will buy a new one.

7.3.6.2   Conjugation

		cantar	vender	partir	pôr
eu	tiver				
tu	tiveres				
ele, ela, você	tiver				
nós	tivermos	cantado	vendido	partido	posto
(vós)	tiverdes				
eles, elas, vocês	tiverem				

7.4   IMPERATIVE MOOD

7.4.1   Conjugation[B]

The Imperative mood expresses commands. In the affirmative, it has only three persons (**tu**, **nós**, **vós**). In all other cases, including the negative, commands are expressed by forms borrowed from the Present Subjunctive. It is presented here conjugated together with the borrowed forms of the Present Subjunctive (in parentheses) for easier consultation:

		cantar	vender	partir	pôr
Positive					
eu		-	-	-	-
tu		canta	vende	parte	põe
você		(cante)	(venda)	(parta)	(ponha)
nós		cantemos	vendamos	partamos	ponhamos
(vós)		cantai	vendei	parti	ponde
vocês		(cantem)	(vendam)	(partam)	(ponham)
Negative					
eu	*não*	-	-	-	-
tu	*não*	(cantes)	(vendas)	(partas)	(ponhas)
você	*não*	(cante)	(venda)	(parta)	(ponha)
nós	*não*	(cantemos)	(vendamos)	(partamos)	(ponhamos)
(vós)	*não*	(canteis)	(vendais)	(partais)	(ponhais)
vocês	*não*	(cantem)	(vendam)	(partam)	(ponham)

7.4.2   Irregular Imperative

ser	sê, sejamos, sede
estar	está, estejamos, estai

ir	vai, vamos, ide
dar	dá, demos, dai
dizer	diz, digamos, dizei
ler	lê, leiamos, lede
ver	vê, vejamos, vede
fazer	faz, façamos, fazei
trazer	traz, tragamos, trazei
saber	sabe, saibamos, sabei

7.5 INFINITIVE

7.5.1 Impersonal Infinitive

The Impersonal Infinitive in the four conjugations ends in **-ar**, **-er**, **-ir** or **-or**:

cant*ar*	**vend*er***	**part*ir***	**p*ôr***

7.5.2 Personal Infinitive

	cant*ar*	**vend*er***	**part*ir***	**p*ôr***
eu	cantar	vender	partir	pôr
tu	cantar*es*	vender*es*	partir*es*	por*es*
ele, ela, você	cantar	vender	partir	pôr
nós	cantar*mos*	vender*mos*	partir*mos*	por*mos*
(vós)	cantar*des*	vender*des*	partir*des*	por*des*
eles, elas, vocês	cantar*em*	vender*em*	partir*em*	por*em*

Note: With regular verbs, the Personal Infinitive and the Future Subjunctive happen to have the same forms. This is not the case with irregular verbs (e.g. **fazer: tu fazeres/tu fizeres**).

7.5.3 Although we can often use either the Impersonal or the Personal Infinitive, the latter is preferred when indicating more clearly the person to whom the Infinitive refers. Especially after **ao** ('when; on doing something') and **para** ('for; in order to'), the Personal Infinitive is used to avoid ambiguity:

Ao *abrir* a porta, eles viram-me.
(Who *opened* the door – did they or did I?)

Ao *abrirem* a porta, eles viram-me.
When *they opened* the door, they saw me.

Isto é para *traduzir* hoje.
(Who has to *translate* it today?)

Isto é para *traduzires* hoje.
This is for you to *translate* today.

7.5.4 In colloquial Portuguese, the Personal Infinitive replaces a subjunctive clause in the following situations:

para que + Subjunctive = **para** + Personal Infinitive
sem que + Subjunctive = **sem** + Personal Infinitive

Vim falar contigo *para que me dês* um conselho.
Vim falar contigo *para me dares um conselho.*
I came to talk to you for some advice.

Nós saímos *sem que eles vissem.*
Nós saímos *sem eles verem.*
We left without being seen (by them).

7.6   PRESENT PARTICIPLE

cant*ar*	**vend*er***	**part*ir***	**p*ôr***
cant*ando*	vend*endo*	part*indo*	p*ondo*

The Present Participle is used in Brazilian Portuguese to express the Progressive tenses. In European Portuguese, **estar a** or **andar a** + Infinitive is preferred:

Eu estou a trabalhar.   I am working.
Eu ando a aprender português.   I am learning Portuguese.

instead of

Estou trabalhando.
Estou estudando português.

But when the English 'to be + -ing' is used to express a future action, it cannot be translated with the Portuguese Progressive. The simple Present tense is used instead:

Ele parte amanhã.   He is leaving tomorrow.
Eles ficam três dias.   They are staying three days.

Note: Contrary to English usage, the Portuguese gerund cannot act as a noun. Where English uses the '-ing' form, Portuguese uses an Infinitive:

Viajar de avião é caro.   Travelling by plane is expensive.

7.7   COMPOUND INFINITIVE AND COMPOUND PRESENT PARTICIPLE

Compound Infinitive **ter** + Past Participle
('having' + Past Participle)

Compound Present Participle **tendo** + Past Participle
('having' + Past Participle)

The Compound Infinitive is normally used after a preposition (**de**, **para**, **por**), while the Compound Present Participle never follows a preposition:

Depois de *ter terminado* o curso, a Isabel voltou para Portugal.
After *having finished* her degree, Isabel returned to Portugal.

***Tendo terminado* o curso, a Isabel voltou para Portugal.**
Having finished her degree, Isabel returned to Portugal.

7.8   PAST PARTICIPLE

cant*ar*	vend*er*	part*ir*	p*ôr*
cant*ado*	vend*ido*	part*ido*	p*osto*

7.8.1   Irregular Past Participle

A few verbs have an irregular Past Participle:

abrir	aberto	*fazer*	feito
cobrir	coberto	*pagar*	pago
dizer	dito	*ver*	visto
escrever	escrito	*vir*	vindo

Note: Some verbs have two Past Participles, one regular and one irregular. The regular form is used when the auxiliary verbs is **ter** or **haver**, and the irregular form when the auxiliary verb is **ser** or **estar**:

	ter/haver	*ser/estar*	
aceitar	**aceitado**	**aceito/aceite**	to accept
entregar	**entregado**	**entregue**	to hand over; to deliver
expulsar	**expulsado**	**expulso**	to expel
matar	**matado**	**morto**	to kill
salvar	**salvado**	**salvo**	to save
soltar	**soltado**	**solto**	to release

acender	**acendido**	**aceso**	to light; to switch on
eleger	**elegido**	**eleito**	to elect
morrer	**morrido**	**morto**	to die
prender	**prendido**	**preso**	to arrest
romper	**rompido**	**roto**	to tear
suspender	**suspendido**	**suspenso**	to hang
exprimir	**exprimido**	**expresso**	to express
extinguir	**extinguido**	**extinto**	to extinguish
imprimir	**imprimido**	**impresso**	to print

7.9 PASSIVE VOICE

ser (in required tense)   + Past Participle   +   **por**
to be   + Past Participle   +   by

The Passive voice in Portuguese is not too different from that of English in its formation and use. It can be used to replace the Active voice.

But in Portuguese, the Past Participle agrees in gender and in number with the subject of the passive sentence, and the preposition **por** contracts with the definite articles **o**, **a**, **os**, as: **pelo**, **pela**, **pelos**, **pelas**:

Os bombeiros *apagam* incêndios.
Firemen *put out* fires.

Os incêndios *são apagados* pelos bombeiros.
Fires *are put out* by firemen.

The Passive voice can be used in all tenses. Here are a few examples:

Present Perfect
Os incêndios têm sido apagados pelos bombeiros.

Imperfect
Os incêndios eram apagados pelos bombeiros.

Past Perfect
Os incêndios tinham sido apagados pelos bombeiros.

Pluperfect
Os incêndios foram apagados pelos bombeiros.

Future
Os incêndios serão apagados pelos bombeiros.

Conditional
Os incêndios seriam apagados pelos bombeiros.

Present Subjunctive
É preciso que os incêndios sejam apagados pelos bombeiros.

Past Subjunctive
Era preciso que os incêndios fossem apagados pelos bombeiros.

Past Perfect Subjunctive
Era preciso que os incêndios tivessem sido apagados pelos bombeiros.

Future Subjunctive
Se os incêndios forem apagados pelos bombeiros ...

Personal Infinitive
É fácil os incêndios serem apagados pelos bombeiros.

7.10 AUXILIARY VERBS

Eu *tenho* feito muito exercício.
I*'ve been* doing a lot of exercise.

***Temos de* ir às compras.**
We *must* go shopping.

***Havemos-de* ir a Paris no Verão.**
We *shall* go to Paris next summer.

Ele *foi* comido por um tubarão.
He *was* eaten by a shark.

Eu *estava a* ouvir música.
I *was* listening to music.

O navio *vai* partir.
The boat *is going to* leave.

***Viemos* visitar-te.**
We *came* to see you.

ter	*haver*	*ser*	*estar*	*ir*	*vir*

INDICATIVE
Present

ter	*haver*	*ser*	*estar*	*ir*	*vir*
tenho	hei	sou	estou	vou	venho
tens	hás	és	estás	vais	vens
tem	há	é	está	vai	vem
temos	havemos	somos	estamos	vamos	vimos
tendes	haveis	sois	estais	ides	vindes
têm	hão	são	estão	vão	vêm

Imperfect

tinha	havia	era	estava	ia	vinha
tinhas	havias	eras	estavas	ias	vinhas
tinha	havia	era	estava	ia	vinha
tínhamos	havíamos	éramos	estávamos	íamos	vínhamos
tínheis	havíeis	éreis	estáveis	íeis	vínheis
tinham	haviam	eram	estavam	iam	vinham

Preterite

tive	houve	fui	estive	fui	vim
tiveste	houveste	foste	estiveste	foste	vieste
teve	houve	foi	esteve	foi	veio
tivemos	houvemos	fomos	estivemos	fomos	viemos
tivestes	houvestes	fostes	estivestes	fostes	viestes
tiveram	houveram	foram	estiveram	foram	vieram

Pluperfect

tivera	houvera	fora	estivera	fora	viera
tiveras	houveras	foras	estiveras	foras	vieras
tivera	houvera	fora	estivera	fora	viera
tivéramos	houvéramos	fôramos	estivéramos	fôramos	viéramos
tivéreis	houvéreis	fôreis	estivéreis	fôreis	viéreis
tiveram	houveram	foram	estiveram	foram	vieram

Future

terei	haverei	serei	estarei	irei	virei
terás	haverás	serás	estarás	irás	virás
terá	haverá	será	estará	irá	virá
teremos	haveremos	seremos	estaremos	iremos	viremos
tereis	havereis	sereis	estareis	ireis	vireis
terão	haverão	serão	estarão	irão	virão

Conditional

teria	haveria	seria	estaria	iria	viria
terias	haverias	serias	estarias	irias	virias
teria	haveria	seria	estaria	iria	viria
teríamos	haveríamos	seríamos	estaríamos	iríamos	viríamos
teríeis	haveríeis	seríeis	estaríeis	iríeis	viríeis
teriam	haveriam	seriam	estariam	iriam	viriam

SUBJUNCTIVE
Present

tenha	haja	seja	esteja	vá	venha
tenhas	hajas	sejas	estejas	vás	venhas
tenha	haja	seja	esteja	vá	venha
tenhamos	hajamos	sejamos	estejamos	vamos	venhamos
tenhais	hajais	sejais	estejais	vades	venhais
tenham	hajam	sejam	estejam	vão	venham

Imperfect

tivesse	houvesse	fosse	estivesse	fosse	viesse
tivesses	houvesses	fosses	estivesses	fosses	viesses
tivesse	houvesse	fosse	estivesse	fosse	viesse
tivéssemos	houvéssemos	fôssemos	estivéssemos	fôssemos	viéssemos
tivésseis	houvésseis	fôsseis	estivésseis	fôsseis	viésseis
tivessem	houvessem	fossem	estivessem	fossem	viessem

Future

tiver	houver	for	estiver	for	vier
tiveres	houveres	fores	estiveres	fores	vieres
tiver	houver	for	estiver	for	vier
tivermos	houvermos	formos	estivermos	formos	viermos
tiverdes	houverdes	fordes	estiverdes	fordes	vierdes
tiverem	houverem	forem	estiverem	forem	vierem

IMPERATIVE
Affirmative

–	–	–	–	–	–
tem	–	sê	está	vai	vem
(tenha)	(haja)	(seja)	(esteja)	(vá)	(venha)
tenhamos	hajamos	sejamos	estejamos	vamos	venhamos
tende	havei	sede	estai	ide	vinde
(tenham)	(hajam)	(sejam)	(estejam)	(vão)	(venham)

Negative

	–	–	–	–	–	–
	tenhas	hajas	sejas	estejas	vás	venhas
não {	tenha	haja	seja	esteja	vá	venha
	tenhamos	hajamos	sejamos	estejamos	vamos	venhamos
	tenhais	hajais	sejais	estejais	vades	venhais
	tenham	hajam	sejam	estejam	vão	venham

INFINITIVES
Impersonal Infinitive

ter	haver	ser	estar	ir	vir

Personal Infinitive

ter	haver	ser	estar	ir	vir
teres	haveres	seres	estares	ires	vires
ter	haver	ser	estar	ir	vir
termos	havermos	sermos	estarmos	irmos	virmos
terdes	haverdes	serdes	estardes	irdes	virdes
terem	haverem	serem	estarem	irem	virem

PARTICIPLES
Present Participle

| tendo | havendo | sendo | estando | indo | vindo |

Past Participle

| tido | havido | sido | estado | ido | vindo |

7.11   IMPERSONAL, UNIPERSONAL AND DEFECTIVE VERBS

7.11.1   Impersonal verbs

Impersonal verbs do not have a subject and are invariably used in the third person singular. They are usually related to nature:

amanhecer	to dawn	**relampejar**	to lighten
anoitecer	to grow dark	**saraivar**	to hail
chover	to rain	**trovejar**	to thunder
chuviscar	to drizzle	**ventar**	to storm
nevar	to snow		

7.11.2   Unipersonal verbs

Unipersonal verbs are only used in the third person singular or the third person plural:

acontecer	to happen	**ganir**	to whine (a dog)
constar	to be rumoured	**ladrar**	to bark
convir	to be convenient	**zumbir**	to buzz
galopar	to gallop	**zurrar**	to bray

7.11.3   Defective verbs

Defective verbs are not conjugated in all tenses. There are two groups of defective verbs.

7.11.3.1   Some verbs such as **abolir**, **aturdir**, **banir**, **colorir**, **demolir**, **emergir**, and **imergir** are not conjugated in:

• first person singular and plural of the Present Indicative;
• Present Subjunctive;
• third person singular of the Imperative;
• first and second person plural of the Imperative.

7.11.3.2 Some verbs, such as **adequar**, **falir**, **precaver-se** and **reaver** are not conjugated in:

- first, second and third persons singular of the Present Indicative;
- third person plural of the Present Indicative;
- Present Subjunctive;
- Imperative, except in the second person plural.

7.12   REFLEXIVE VERBS[B]

eu	lavo-*me*	nós[1]	lavamo-*nos*
tu	lavas-*te*	(vós)	lavais-*vos*
ele, ela, você	lava-*se*	eles, elas, vocês	lavam-*se*

[1] When the reflexive pronoun is placed after the second person plural of the verb, the verb loses its final **-s** (e.g. **nós lavamos = nós lavamo-nos**).

7.12.1   Position of the reflexive pronoun

7.12.1.1 The reflexive pronoun is usually placed after the verb (linked to it by a hyphen) except in negative and interrogative sentences, after conjunctions, prepositions or relative clauses (see 5.1.2.1 and 5.1.2.2).

7.12.1.2 When the verb with the reflexive pronoun stands with an auxiliary, the pronoun can follow the main verb or the auxiliary (more colloquial):[B]

Posso *sentar-me* aqui?   May I sit here?
***Posso-me* sentar aqui?**   Can I sit here?

7.12.1.3 In the Indicative Future or Conditional, the reflexive pronoun is placed between the stem and the ending of the verb, with each part separated by hyphens:[B]

Future	*Future Perfect*	*Conditional*	*Conditional Perfect*
lavar-*me*-ei	ter-*me*-ei lavado	lavar-*me*-ia	ter-*me*-ia lavado
lavar-*te*-ás	ter-*te*-ás lavado	lavar-*te*-ias	ter-*te*-ias lavado
lavar-*se*-á	ter-*se*-á lavado	lavar-*se*-ia	ter-*se*-ia lavado
lavar-*nos*-emos	ter-*nos*-emos lavado	lavar-*nos*-íamos	ter-*nos*-íamos lavado
lavar-*vos*-eis	ter-*vos*-eis lavado	lavar-*vos*-íeis	ter-*vos*-íeis lavado
lavar-*se*-ão	ter-*se*-ão lavado	lavar-*se*-iam	ter-*se*-iam lavado

7.12.1.4 The reflexive pronouns can be supplemented with **um ao outro**, **uma à outra** or **uns aos outros**, to avoid confusion:

Estes peixes comem-*se*.
These fish are edible. *or* These fish eat each other.

Estes peixes comem-*se uns aos outros*.
These fish eat each other.

7.12.2 Here are the Infinitives of some of the most commonly used reflexive verbs:

achar-se	to find oneself	**banhar-se**	to bathe
amar-se	to love each other	**barbear-se**	to shave
apaixonar-se	to fall in love	**chamar-se**	to be called
beijar-se	to kiss each other	**lavar-se**	to wash
deitar-se	to go to bed, to lie down	**sentar-se**	to sit down
levantar-se	to stand up, to get up	**sentir-se**	to feel
pentear-se	to comb one's hair	**voltar-se**	to turn around

7.13 CHANGING VOWEL SOUNDS IN VERBAL CONJUGATION

In many Portuguese verbs, the sound of the stem vowel changes in the Present Indicative, Present Subjunctive and the Imperative:

Present Indicative		*Present Subjunctive*		*Imperative*	

First conjugation (-ar verbs)

open	**la*v*o**	open	**la*v*e**	–	–
open	**la*v*as**	open	**la*v*es**	open	**la*v*a**
open	**la*v*a**	open	**la*v*e**	open	**la*v*e**
	lavamos		lavemos		lavemos
	lavais		lavemos		lavai
open	**la*v*am**	open	**la*v*em**	open	**la*v*em**

Note: In the first conjugation, the stem vowel is closed in all other tenses.

Second conjugation (-er verbs)

closed	**de*v*o**	closed	**de*v*a**	–	–
open	**de*v*es**	closed	**de*v*as**	open	**de*v*e**
open	**de*v*e**	closed	**de*v*a**	closed	**de*v*a**
	devemos		devamos		devamos
	deveis		devais		devei
open	**de*v*em**	closed	**de*v*am**	closed	**de*v*am**

Present Indicative   *Present Subjunctive*   *Imperative*

Third conjugation (-ir verbs)

u	d*u*rmo	u	d*u*rma		
open	d*o*rmes	u	d*u*rmas	open	d*o*rme
open	d*o*rme	u	d*u*rma	u	d*u*rma
	d*o*rmimos	u	d*u*rmamos	u	d*u*rmamos
	d*o*rmis	u	d*u*rmais		d*o*rmi
open	d*o*rmem	u	d*u*rmam	u	d*u*rmam

Note: In the first, second and third conjugations, the stem vowel is unstressed in all other tenses.

8 ADVERBS

8.1 USES OF THE ADVERB

Adverbs can act as modifiers of a verb, an adjective, another adverb or a whole sentence:

Ontem fui a Lisboa.
I went to Lisbon *yesterday*.

Ele é *bem* simpático.
He is *quite* nice.

Elas foram *muito* depressa.
They went *very* quickly.

Infelizmente choveu o dia todo.
Unfortunately it rained all day long.

Adverbs are invariable: that is, they do not vary according to the gender, number or person of the word they are modifying.

Adverbs can be used to express:

(a) *time*: **ontem** ('yesterday'), **hoje** ('today'), **amanhã** ('tomorrow'), **antes** ('before'), **depois** ('after'), **agora** ('now'), **já** ('already, straight away'), **logo** ('later'), **cedo** ('early'), **tarde** ('late'), **então** ('then'), **ainda** ('yet, still'), **enfim** ('at last'), **breve** ('soon'), **sempre** ('always'), **de vez em quando** ('once in a while').

(b) *place*: **aqui, cá** ('here'), **aí, ali, lá, acolá,** ('there'), **perto** ('near'), **longe** ('far'), **diante, à frente de** ('in front of'), **atrás, detrás** ('behind'), **acima** ('above'), **em cima** ('on'), **por cima** ('over'), **abaixo** ('below'), **em baixo, por baixo** ('under'), **dentro** ('in, inside'), **fora** ('out, outside'), **onde** ('where'), **algures** ('somewhere').

Note: Adverbs of place are either used with reference to the position of the speaker and/or the hearer:

aqui	nearness to the speaker
aí	nearness to the hearer
ali	distance from both speaker and hearer
cá	nearness to the speaker without reference to the position of the hearer
lá, acolá, além	distance from the speaker without reference to the position of the hearer

(c) *manner*: **bem** ('well'), **mal** ('badly'), **assim** ('thus'), **depressa** ('quickly'), **devagar** ('slowly') and most adverbs ending in **-mente** (see 8.2).

(d) *intensity*: **pouco** ('little'), **muito** ('very'), **menos** ('less'), **demasiado** ('too much'), **quanto?** ('how much?'), **tanto** ('as much'), **tão** ('so'), **mais** ('more'), **demais** ('too much, too many'), **bastante** ('enough'), **quase** ('almost').

(e) *doubt*: **talvez** ('perhaps, maybe'), **por acaso** ('by chance'), **possivelmente** ('possibly'), **provavelmente** ('probably').

(f) *negation*: **não** ('no'), **nem** ('nor'), **nunca** ('never'), **jamais** ('never ever').

(g) *affirmation*: **sim** ('yes'), **certamente** ('certainly'), **realmente** ('really').

(h) *exclusion*: **só, somente** ('only'), **unicamente** ('merely'), **simplesmente** ('simply'), **exclusivamente** ('exclusively'), **apenas** ('just, hardly').

(i) *interrogation*: **onde?** ('where?'), **como?** ('how?'), **porquê?** ('why?'), **quando?** ('when?').

8.2 ADVERBS IN -MENTE

In Portuguese, many adverbs are formed by adding the suffix **-mente** ('-ly') to the adjective:

normal	**normalmente**	normal	normally

But adjectives ending in **-o** in the masculine singular change to the feminine singular before the suffix **-mente** is added:

lento > lenta	**lentamente**	slow	slowly

There are two important characteristics of adverbs in **-mente**:

(a) Adverbs in **-mente** have no accents, even if the adjective from which they are formed does:

fácil	**facilmente**	easy	easily

(b) When two or more adverbs are used in the same sentence, only the last one takes the suffix **-mente**:

Ele guiava lenta e cuidadosamente.
He was driving slowly and carefully.

8.3   OTHER ADVERBS

The adjectives **muito** ('a lot'), **pouco** ('little'), **demasiado** ('too much'), **melhor** ('better') and **pior** ('worse') can also be adverbs, if qualifying a verb:

Ela trabalha muito.	She works a lot.
Ele come demasiado.	He eats too much.
Pouco se sabe deste compositor.	Little is known of this composer.

Adverbs may also consist of more than one word:

preposition + noun	**sem dúvida**	doubtlessly
preposition + adjective	**ao certo**	exactly
preposition + adverb	**pelo menos**	at least
two adverbs	**nunca mais**	never again

8.4   POSITION

8.4.1   Usually adverbs are placed before the adjective or after the verb they modify:

Que festa tão animada!	What a lively party!
Ela chorou desesperadamente.	She cried desperately.

8.4.2   Adverbs of time and place can either precede or follow the verb they modify:

Ele chegou hoje.	He arrived today.
Hoje quero ficar aqui.	Today I want to stay here.

8.4.3   Adverbs of negation always precede the verb:

Ela nunca tinha feito isso.	She had never done that.
Não há pão.	There is no bread.

8.5   DEGREE

8.5.1   Comparative

comparative of superiority	**mais** + adverb + **(do) que**
	more . . . than
comparative of equality	**tão** + adverb + **como/quanto**
	as . . . as
comparative of inferiority	**menos** + adverb + **(do) que**
	less . . . than

Eu vivo *mais longe do que* tu.
I live *further away than* you.

Ela vive *tão longe quanto* eu.
She lives *as far away as* I do.

Tu vives *menos longe do que* nós.
You live *closer than* we do.

Note: There are adverbs with special comparative forms:

bem	> **melhor**	well	better
mal	> **pior**	badly	worse
muito	> **mais**	a lot	more
pouco	> **menos**	little	less

Adverbs can be compared using **o mais** + adverb + **possível**:

Vou o mais depressa possível.   I'll go as fast as I can.

8.5.2   Superlative

Adverb (minus final vowel) + **-íssimo**

Cantas muitíssimo bem.   You sing very well.
Ela mora pertíssimo.   She lives very near.

9 CONJUNCTIONS

9.1 CO-ORDINATING CONJUNCTIONS

Co-ordinating conjunctions link clauses of identical grammatical function:

Ela brinca *e* eu estudo.	She plays *and* I study.
Ela brinca *mas* eu estudo.	She plays *but* I study.

The two elements of these clauses are independent of each other and could even be separated by punctuation:

Ela brinca, eu estudo.	She plays; I study.
Ela brinca. Eu estudo.	She plays. I study.

9.1.1 Copulative conjunctions

e	and
não só ... mas também	not only ... but also
nem ... nem	neither ... nor
tanto ... como	both ... and

O João é alto *e* magro.
João is tall *and* thin.

Ele não tem *nem* dinheiro *nem* trabalho.
He has *neither* money *nor* job.

Vim *não só* porque me pediste *mas também* porque eu queria ver este filme.
I came *not only* because you asked me to *but also* because I wanted to see this film.

Tanto a Helena *como* o irmão já sabem ler.
Both Helena and her brother can already read.

9.1.2 Adversative conjunctions

mas	but	**todavia**	yet
porém	however	**contudo**	nevertheless

Tropecei *mas* não caí.
I stumbled *but* I did not fall.

O dia estava bonito, *porém/contudo/todavia* **não fui passear.**
It was a lovely day, *however/yet/nevertheless* I did not go for a walk.

9.1.3   Disjunctive conjunctions

| **ou** | or | **quer ... quer** | whether ... or |
| **ou ... ou** | either ... or | **nem ... nem** | neither ... nor |

Vens *ou* **ficas?**
Are you coming *or* are you staying?

Ou **comes peixe** *ou* **comes carne.**
You eat *either* fish *or* meat.

Quer **tu queiras** *quer* **não, tens de te ir embora.**
Whether you want to *or* not, you must leave.

9.1.4   Conclusive conjunctions

portanto	therefore; so	**por consequência**	consequently
logo	therefore; so	**por conseguinte**	consequently
por isso	therefore; so	**pelo que**	consequently
assim	thus		

Não me estou a sentir bem, *por isso* **não vou à escola.**
I am not feeling well, *so* I am not going to school.

Note: Conclusive conjunctions are normally placed at the beginning of the clause they introduce.

9.2   SUBORDINATING CONJUNCTIONS

Subordinating conjunctions link two clauses necessarily dependent on each other:

Eu estava a ler *quando* **ele entrou.**
I was reading *when* he came in.

9.2.1   Causal conjunctions

porque	because	**visto que**	seeing that
pois	because	**já que**	since
que	because	**uma vez que**	since
como	as		

Não telefonei *porque* **não tive tempo.**
I did not call *because* I did not have the time.

Como **estava a chover ficámos em casa.**
As it was raining we stayed in.

9.2.2 Concessive conjunctions

embora	although	**mesmo que**	even if; even though
apesar de	despite; in spite of	**por mais que**	as much as
ainda que	even if; even though	**nem que**	not even if

Apesar de **estar um dia bonito não fui passear.**
Despite/in spite of it being a lovely day I did not go for a walk.

Por mais que **tentes, não me convences a ir de avião.**
As much as you try, you will not convince me to go by plane.

9.2.3 Conditional conjunctions

se	if	**excepto se**	unless
caso	if	**salvo se**	unless
desde que	provided that	**a não ser que**	unless
a menos que	provided that		

A *não ser que* **chova, fazemos um piquenique amanhã.**
Unless it rains, we will have a picnic tomorrow.

Note: Conditional conjunctions take the verb either in the Infinitive or in the Subjunctive.

9.2.4 Final conjunctions

para que	so that	**a fim de que**	in order to

Aproxima-te *para que* **eu te possa ver melhor.**
Come closer *so that* I can see you better.

Note: These conjunctions must be followed by the Subjunctive.

9.2.5 Temporal conjunctions

quando	when	**antes que**	before
apenas	as soon as	**depois que**	after
mal	as soon as; hardly	**sempre que**	whenever
logo que	as soon as	**desde que**	since
assim que	as soon as	**enquanto**	while

Quando **eu cheguei, ele já lá estava.**
When I arrived, he was already there.

Enquanto **ela lia o jornal, o marido via televisão.**
While she was reading the paper, her husband watched television.

9.2.6 Comparative conjunctions

como	as	**bem como**	as well as
que nem	as	**assim como**	as well as
... do que	... than	**como se**	as if
tanto quanto	as much as; as far as		

Sei mais agora *do que* sabia há uns anos atrás.
I know more now *than* I knew a few years ago.

Ele fala *como se* fosse meu pai.
He speaks *as if* he were my father.

9.2.7 Consecutive conjunctions

tal que	
tanto que	
de tal maneira que	in such a way that
de tal modo que	

O rapaz caiu *de tal maneira que* teve que ser levado para o hospital.
The boy fell *in such a way that* he had to be taken to hospital.

9.2.8 Integrating conjunctions

que	that	**se**	if

A Maria disse *que* também vinha connosco.
Maria said *that* she was also coming with us.

Note: Subordinating conjunctions are placed at the beginning of the clause they introduce.

10 PREPOSITIONS

10.1 PREPOSITIONS

a	to	em	in
ante	before	entre	between
após	after	excepto	except
até	until	para	for; to
com	with	perante	in the presence
conforme	according to		of; before
consoante	according to	por	by
contra	against	sob	under
de	of	sobre	over
desde	from	sem	without
durante	during		

10.2 PREPOSITIONAL PHRASES

abaixo de	below	apesar de	despite; in spite
por baixo de	under		of
acima de	above	a fim de	in order to
por cima de	on; over	antes de	before
em cima de	on	depois de	after
ao lado de	next to	diante de	in front of
além de	beyond	atrás de	behind
acerca de	about	longe de	away from
ao redor de	around	através de	through
em torno de	around	dentro de	inside; in
perto de	near	a respeito de	concerning
próximo de	near; close to	junto de	near
para com	towards	de acordo com	in accordance
por entre	through; amongst		with;
fora de	outside; out of		accordingly
ao longo de	along	em frente de	in front of
de cima de	from the top of	graças a	thanks to
ao pé de	next to; nearby		
em vez de	instead; in		
	place of		

10.3 CONTRACTION OF PREPOSITION + ARTICLE OR PRONOUN

See 3.4 on contraction of the definite article, 3.8 on contraction of the indefinite article, and 5.3.2 and 5.3.3 on demonstratives combined with prepositions.

10.4 VERBS FOLLOWED BY A PREPOSITION[B]

olhar para	to look at	**entrar em**	to go into; to enter
assistir a	to attend; to watch	**chegar a**	to arrive at; to reach
encontrar-se com	to meet	**ir a, para**	to go to
casar-se com	to marry	**ir de**	to go by (transport)
mudar de	to change from	**vir a, para**	to come to
sorrir para	to smile at	**vir de**	to come by (transport)
rir de	to laugh at		

Some verbs followed by a preposition take a verb in the Infinitive:

ajudar a	to help to	**gostar de**	to like to
começar a	to start to; to begin to	**pensar em**	to think about
acabar de	to finish; to have just	**pedir para**	to ask to
		precisar de	to need

lembrar-se de	to remember
esquecer-se de	to forget

Ajude-me a lavar o carro.
Help me wash the car.

O António acaba de sair.
António has just left.

Você esqueceu-se de apagar a luz.
You forgot to turn off the light.

Gosto de aprender português.
I enjoy learning Portuguese.

Peço-lhe para prestar atenção.
I am asking you to pay attention.

Preciso de ir ao supermercado.
I need to go to the supermarket.

11 ADDITIONAL NOTES ON PORTUGUESE USAGE

11.1 GENTE/A GENTE

Gente means 'people' and it may correspond to **pessoas**. It takes a verb in the third person singular:

Aonde vai aquela gente toda?
Where are all those people going?

O café estava cheio de gente.
The café was full of people.

A gente do Porto é muito simpática.
The people of Oporto are very nice.

A gente may be used in the sense of **nós** in very colloquial speech. It is followed by a verb in the third person singular:[B]

– **Aonde é que vocês vão?**
Where are you going?

– **A gente vai ao cinema. (Nós vamos ao cinema.)**
We're going to the cinema.

11.2 TUDO/TODO

Tudo is invariable and means 'everything' or 'all'. It can be used with **isto**, **isso** and **aquilo** but never with a noun:

Tens que comer tudo.	You must eat everything.
Tens que comer isso tudo.	You must eat it all.

Todo is variable (**todo/a/os/as**), agreeing in gender and number with the noun it qualifies. It means 'all' or 'every' and is never used with **isto**, **isso** or **aquilo**:

Tens que comer as batatas todas.
You must eat all the potatoes.

Note: The degree of emphasis is increased if **todo/a/os/as** is placed immediately after the verb:

Tens que comer todas as batatas.
You must eat every single potato.

11.3   POR/PARA

Both **por** and **para** can be translated as 'for' but with different meanings:

(a) **Por** is used to convey the idea of:

Exchange
   Paguei 100$00 pelo café.
   I paid Esc.100 for the coffee.

Substitution
   Vou trocar estes sapatos pretos por uns castanhos.
   I am going to change these black shoes for some brown ones.

Duration
   Por quanto tempo vais ficar em Itália?
   (For) How long are you going to stay in Italy?

Note: Remember that the preposition **por** contracts with the definite article (see 3.4.1.4).

(b) **Para** conveys the idea of

Destination
   Isto é para si.
   This is for you.

11.4   A/PARA

Both **a** and **para** convey the idea of movement towards, but **a** implies a short stay whereas **para** implies a relatively long or permanent stay:[B]

   Eu vou ao Brasil em viagem de negócios.
   I am going to Brazil on business (and I am coming back soon).

   Eu vou para o Brasil.
   I am going to Brazil (one assumes that I do not know when I am coming back).

11.5   DESDE ... ATÉ/DE ... A

Desde and **de** are used to express the starting point of a period of time or space:

   Venho desde Leiria com os pneus em baixo.
   Since Leiria my tyres have been going down.

   De Maio em diante não há mais autocarros.
   There are no buses from May onwards.

The endpoint of this period of time or space is expressed by **até** or **a**, where **desde** combines with **até** and **de** combines with **a**:

desde Janeiro até Junho	from January to June
or	
de Janeiro a Junho	
desde as 9 até às 5	from 9 to 5
or	
das 9 às 5	
desde Braga até Guimarães	from Braga to Guimarães
or	
de Braga a Guimarães	

The difference between usage is that **desde ... até** is more emphatic:

O quê? Ele foi mesmo a pé desde Braga até Guimarães?
What? Did he really walk from Braga to Guimarães?

11.6   PRÓXIMO/SEGUINTE

Both **próximo** and **seguinte** mean 'next'. However, the difference between them lies in their point of reference: **próximo** means 'next' in relation to the present moment, whereas **seguinte** means 'next' in relation to a given point in the past or future.

Therefore, **próximo** is used in direct speech and **seguinte** is normally used in reported speech (and can be translated as 'the following'):

No próximo mês não há aulas.
There will not be any classes next month.

Em Julho avisei que não havia aulas no mês seguinte.
In July I said that there would be no classes the following month.

11.7   TÃO/TANTO

Tão is invariable and can be used before an adjective or an adverb:

Esta paisagem é tão bonita!	This landscape is so pretty!
Não comas tão depressa!	Don't eat so quickly!

Tanto is variable when placed before a noun (it agrees with the noun in gender and number: **tanto/a/os/as**) and invariable when placed after a verb as it refers to intensity:

Ele recebeu tantos presentes!	He got so many presents!
Gosto tanto daquele vestido!	I like that dress so much!

11.8 AFFIRMATIVE/NEGATIVE

The affirmative is usually expressed by **sim**, although this is rarely used on its own. An affirmative answer to a question is given by the verb, which may or may not be preceded or followed by **sim** as reinforcement:

Vais amanhã?	Are you going tomorrow?
Vou.	Yes.
Sim, vou.	Yes, I'm going.
Vou, vou. (less formal)	Yes, I'm going.

The negative is usually expressed by **não** (simple negative), **nem** (reinforced negative), **nunca** or **jamais** (absolute negative; the latter is more commonly used in literary language):

O Pedro não viu esse filme.	Pedro has not seen that film.
O Pedro nem viu esse filme.	Pedro has not even seen that film.
O Pedro nunca viu esse filme.	Pedro never saw that film.
O Pedro jamais viu esse filme.	Pedro never ever saw that film.

11.9 AINDA/JÁ

Ainda usually means 'still', in statements, questions and answers; **ainda não** means 'not yet'. **Já** means 'already'; **já não** means 'not anymore'.

Ainda há pão?	Is there still some bread left?
Sim, ainda há algum.	Yes, there's still some.
Não, já não há nenhum.	No, there is none anymore.
Já há pão?	Is there already some bread?
Sim, já há.	Yes, there's already some.
Não, ainda não há.	No, there is none yet.

11.10 PREPOSITIONS OF TIME

a	aos domingos	on Sundays
	às 7 horas	at seven o'clock
	à tarde, à noite	in the afternoon, in the/at night
de	de manhã, de tarde, de noite[1]	in the/during the morning; during the afternoon; during the night
	das 9 às 5	from 9 to 5
em	no sábado passado	last Saturday
	em Junho	in June
	no Natal	at Christmas
	na Primavera	in Spring
para	às 5 para as 7	at 5 to 7 (i.e. 6.55 a.m.)

[1] We can say **à tarde** or **de tarde**, **à noite** or **de noite** but we can only say **de manhã**.

Note: Remember that the prepositions **de**, **a** and **em** are contracted with the definite article (see 3.4).

11.11 PREPOSITIONS WITH MEANS OF TRANSPORT

de	**carro, autocarro, metropolitano**	by car, bus, underground, coach,
	(metro), camioneta, táxi,	taxi, tram, boat, plane,
	eléctrico, barco, avião,	train, donkey
	comboio, burro	
a	**pé, cavalo**	on foot, horseback

But **em** is used when the means of transport is specified:

no carro do meu pai	in my father's car
no autocarro nº 52	in the number 52 bus
no comboio das 11 horas	on the 11 o'clock train
no cavalo da minha prima	on my cousin's horse

11.12 WORD ORDER

11.12.1 Pronouns and verbs[B]

Non-subject pronouns are usually placed after the verb, linked to it by a hyphen:

Ela escreveu-me uma carta.
She wrote me a letter.

Ela telefonou-me e escreveu-me uma carta.[B]
She phoned me and wrote me a letter.

Ela não telefonou, mas/contudo/porém/no entanto escreveu-me uma carta.
She did not phone but wrote me a letter.

Note: With compound tenses, pronouns are placed after the auxiliary verb:

Ela tinha-me escrito uma carta.[B]   She had written me a letter.

Note: With the Future Indicative or the Conditional pronouns are placed between the stem and the ending:

Ela escrever-me-á uma carta.[B]   She will write me a letter.
Ela escrever-me-ia uma carta.[B]   She would write me a letter.

But pronouns are placed before the verb in the following cases:

(a) In negative sentences:

Ela não me escreveu uma carta.
She did not write me a letter.

(b) In sentences beginning with **todo**, **tudo**, **muito**, **pouco**, **alguém**, **cada qual**, **qualquer**, **outro**, **tal**, **tanto**, **quanto**:

Alguém me escreveu uma carta.
Someone wrote me a letter.

Tanto me faz ir ao Japão como à China.
I do not mind going to Japan or China.

(c) In sentences beginning with adverbs:

Já me escreveu uma carta.
She has already written me a letter.

(d) In subordinate clauses:

Disseram-me que ela me tinha escrito uma carta.
They told me that she had written me a letter.

11.12.2   Possessive pronouns and nouns

Possessive pronouns are usually placed before the noun:

O meu carro é branco.   My car is white.

But possessive pronouns are placed after the noun when the noun is accompanied by an indefinite article:

O João é um amigo meu.   João is a friend of mine.

11.12.3   Demonstrative pronouns and nouns

Demonstrative pronouns are usually placed before the noun:

Este edifício tem vinte andares.
This building has twenty floors.

11.12.4   Adjectives and nouns

Adjectives are usually placed after the noun; however, when placed before the noun they can lose their objective meaning:

uma mulher grande   a big woman
uma grande mulher   a great woman

11.12.5   Adverbs

(a) Adverbs are placed before adjectives and participles or may be combined with another adverb (adverbs of intensity precede other adverbs):

uma mulher muito alta   a very tall woman
Ele vinha muito apressado. He was very rushed.
Ela sentiu-se muito mal.   She felt very badly.

(b) Adverbs of manner are placed after verbs:

Ele partiu subitamente.   He left suddenly.

(c) Adverbs of time or place are placed before or after verbs:

Ontem fui a um concerto.
Yesterday I went to a concert.

Fui a um concerto ontem.
I went to a concert yesterday.

À direita fica o castelo de S. Jorge.
On the right is St George's castle.

O castelo de S. Jorge fica à direita.
St George's castle is on the right.

Note: Some adverbs placed before the verb can add emphasis:

Muito se esforça ele para agradar a todos.
He tries very hard to please everybody.

Ela sempre inventa uma desculpa.
She always makes up an excuse.

But the adverb **sempre** can be a sentence adverb if placed before the verb, thus modifying the whole sentence:

Eu viajo sempre de avião.   I always travel by plane.
Eu sempre vou à China.   I am *finally* going to China.

(d) Negative adverbs are placed before verbs:

Ele nunca foi ao teatro.   He has never been to the theatre.

11.12.6 Direct/indirect objects

Objects are usually placed in the following order:

Eu dei *o livro ao Luís*.   verb + direct object + indirect object
                                       I gave *the book to Luis*.

If the direct object is replaced by a pronoun, this order does not change:

Eu dei-*o ao Luís*.   verb + direct object + indirect object
                                       I gave *it to Luis*.

However, if the indirect object or the two objects are replaced by pronouns, their order is altered. In a main clause or a question not introduced by an interrogative, the pronoun is attracted to the verb and linked to it by a hyphen:

Eu dei-*lhe o livro*.   verb + indirect object + direct object
                                       I gave *him the book*.

Eu dei-*lho*. (lhe + o)   verb + [indirect object + direct object]
                               I gave *it to him*.

In a subordinate clause, a question introduced by an interrogative or in the presence of a negative, the pronoun is still attracted to the verb, but precedes it:

Ele diz que eu lhe dei o livro.   subordinate clause + pronoun + verb
Quem lhe deu o livro?   interrogative + pronoun + verb
Eu não lho dei.   negative + pronoun + verb

11.13   SER/ESTAR

Both verbs are translated into English as 'to be', although *they are not* freely interchangeable:

Ser   indicates a state of permanence and inherent qualities or conditions that are unlikely to change (location, nationality, profession, features, demeanour, etc.).

Estar refers to a state or condition that is changeable or likely to change (feelings, moods, change of location, weather conditions, etc.).

O templo de Diana *é* em Évora.
The Temple of Diana *is* in Évora.

Nem todos os Ministérios *estão* no Terreiro do Paço.
Not all Ministries *are* in Terreiro do Paço.

A Paula Rego *é* uma pintora Portuguesa que *está* a viver em Londres.
Paula Rego *is* a Portuguese painter who *is* living in London.

A Judite sempre *foi* muito bonita, mas nas fotografias de casamento *está* linda.
Judite *was* always very pretty, but she *looks* beautiful in her wedding photos.

O João *é* uma pessoa naturalmente nervosa, ou *está* preocupado com os exames?
Is João a naturally nervous person or *is* he worried about his exams?

O Verão no Alentejo *é* geralmente quente, mas este ano *está* abrasador.
Summer in the Alentejo *is* usually hot but this year it *is* scorchingly hot.

PART II: LANGUAGE FUNCTIONS

In an effort to make this section as clear and succinct as possible, the basic expressions are given, followed by a brief explanation and examples often in the form of a short dialogue. As in the previous section, a translation is provided for all examples.

12 SOCIALIZING

12.1 GENERAL GREETINGS

12.1.1 Informal

Olá   Hello!, Hi!

Frequently used for close family, friends and colleagues, **olá** can double up as a sign of recognition, like 'Hi!' in English. The reply is also **Olá!**

Olá!	Hi!
Olá, Joana!	Hello, Joana!
Viva!	Hi!

Used more seldom, **Viva!** expresses delight on seeing someone:

Olá! Por aqui?	Hello! Fancy meeting you here!
Viva! Há quanto tempo!	Hi! It's been a long time!

12.1.2 Formal welcome greeting

Bem-vindo/a/os/as.   Welcome.

Used as a more formal welcome, **Bem-vindo** can be used for friends who have come to stay:

– **Bem-vindos a Viana do Castelo!**
  Welcome to Viana do Castelo!

– **Olá, João! Bem-vindo a nossa casa.**
  Hello, João! Welcome to our house.

Other variations:

dar as *boas-vindas* (a alguém)
apresentar as *boas-vindas* (a alguém) ⎫ to welcome
apresentar votos de *boas-vindas* (a alguém) ⎭ (someone)

A Comissão deseja apresentar as boas-vindas aos novos membros.
The Committee wishes to welcome its new members.

12.2 TAKING LEAVE

12.2.1 Informal

Adeus.   Goodbye.

A general farewell formula, **adeus** can be used on its own or combined
with other farewell formulas. On its own, it implies a longer parting until
speakers meet again.

- **Adeus, boa viagem!**
  Goodbye! Have a good trip!

- **Obrigada. Adeus!**
  Thanks. Goodbye!

- **Adeus, até logo!**
  Bye-bye! See you later!

- **Até logo!**[B]
  Bye!

- **Antes de partir, quero dizer adeus a todos os meus amigos.**
  Before leaving, I want to say goodbye to all my friends.

12.2.1.1 There are other leave-taking formulas which can be used on
their own or combined with **adeus**. Most of these formulas make a statement as to when speakers expect to meet again, and have as their key
element the word **até**, 'until', which in this case has rather the meaning
of 'see you . . . (whenever)'.

Até já!	See you anon, in a minute!
Até logo![B]	See you later!
Até amanhã!	See you tomorrow!
Até depois de amanhã!	See you the day after tomorrow!
Até sábado! (or any day of the week)	See you on Saturday!
Até para a semana!	See you next week!
Até para o mês que vem!	See you next month!
Até para o ano!	See you next year!
Até à próxima!	Until next time!
Até sempre![1]	Until we meet again!

[1] **Até sempre** is also used as a closing formula in letter writing.

12.2.2 More formal farewells, figurative

despedir-se
apresentar despedidas

Quero-me despedir dos teus pais.
I want to say goodbye to your parents.

Desejamos apresentar as nossas despedidas à comissão de recepção e agradecer a agradável estadia que nos proporcionou.
We wish to bid farewell to the Reception Committee and thank them for a wonderful stay.

Coimbra tem mais encanto na hora da despedida.
Coimbra is more charming when you are about to leave.

12.3 GREETING/TAKING LEAVE ACCORDING TO TIME OF DAY

Bom dia!	Good morning!
Boa tarde!	Good afternoon!
Boa noite!	Good evening/night!

These formulas can be used to greet someone, to open a conversation, to attract someone's attention (mostly in shops), or to close a conversation as one is about to leave.

– **Bom dia!**	Good morning!
– **Bom dia!**	Good morning!
– **Tem o _Diário de Notícias_?**	Have you got the _Diário de Notícias_?
– **Não, já só temos _O Público_.**	No, we have only got _O Público_.
– **Prefiro o outro. Bom dia!**	I prefer the other paper. Goodbye!

– **Boa noite! Que horas são?**	Good evening. What time is it?
– **São oito e meia.**	It is 8.30.

12.4 ATTRACTING ATTENTION

As indicated above, any of these greetings (**bom dia**, **boa tarde** and **boa noite**) will do to initiate a conversation or attract attention in a café, a shop, or even to attract the attention of someone in the street who could help you with some information.

If you need to be more obvious, or you are in a crowd, for example in a café, restaurant, market, street, etc., you can use the following formulas:

Faça favor![B]	Excuse me (meaning 'could you please give me/tell me/etc.')
Desculpe	Excuse me
Pst![B,1]	

[1] Can only be used to call a waiter in a café or restaurant. You must never say 'Waiter!' in Portugal. Brazilians say **Garçon!**

Faça favor, têm gravatas de seda?
Excuse me, do you sell silk ties?

Desculpe, onde é o correio?
Excuse me, where is the post office?

Pst! Um café e um copo de água.
Waiter! A cup of coffee and a glass of water.

12.4.1   Asking people to pay attention

Any imperative forms of the verbs **olhar**, **escutar**, or of the idiom **prestar atenção** (see 7.3.1 and 7.4):

Olha!, Olhe!, Olhem!	Look!
Escuta!, Escute!, Escutem!	Listen!
Presta/preste/prestem atenção!	Pay attention!
Olha! Estou aqui.	Look! I am here.
Olhe! Tanta gente!	Look! So many people!
Escute! Isto é importante.	Listen! This is important.
Escuta! Não ouves música?	Listen! Can you hear music?

Preste atenção! Já temos pouco tempo.
Pay attention! We haven't much time.

All these can be emphasized and/or slightly modified by using them with **aqui** or **bem**:

Olha/e aqui!	Look here!
Escuta/e aqui!	Listen carefully!
Escuta/e bem!	Pay good attention!
Escuta/e bem aqui!	Listen really well to what I have to say!

Olha/e bem aqui!
Pay very good attention (do not ignore me, this, etc.)!

Olha aqui! Que significa isto?
Look here! What does this mean?

Olha bem aqui! Afinal, que pretendes?
Look here! What do you really want?

12.4.2   Warning

The following warning words are often used as a sharp cry or shout warning people of danger. They can be followed by instructions which are given with a Subjunctive as they have the function of commands.

Atenção!	Pay attention!
Cuidado!	Watch out! Be careful!
Aviso.	Warning.

Atenção aos comboios!	Watch out for trains!
Pare, escute e olhe!	Stop, listen and look!
Cuidado! Não caias!	Watch out! Don't fall!
Cuidado com o cão.	Beware of the dog.

Aviso	*Notice*
Só se aceita pagamentos em dinheiro.	Payment must be made in cash.

12.4.3 Call for help

Socorro!	Help!	**Acudam!**	Help!
Agarra que é ladrão!	Stop thief!		

12.5 SEASONAL GREETINGS

Feliz Natal!	Merry Christmas!
Boas Festas!	Season's Greetings!
Festas Felizes!	
Feliz Páscoa!	Happy Easter!

12.6 PERSONAL GREETINGS

Parabéns!	Happy birthday!
Feliz aniversário!	Happy birthday/anniversary!

12.7 CONGRATULATIONS

Parabéns!
Congratulations! Happy birthday!

dar os parabéns a (alguém)
to congratulate (someone)

Este ano recebi 10 cartões de parabéns.
This year I received ten birthday cards.

Parabéns por teres passado no exame de condução.
Congratulations on passing your driving test.

Dou-lhe os meus parabéns por um excelente jantar.
I congratulate you on such a wonderful dinner.

12.8 GOOD WISHES

Boas férias!	Have a happy holiday!
Bom fim-de-semana!	Have a good week-end!
Boa viagem!	Have a good trip/journey!

Feliz regresso!	Have a safe journey home!
Boa sorte!	Good luck!

12.9   INTRODUCTIONS

apresentar-se	to introduce oneself
ser apresentado a (alguém)	to be introduced to (someone)
ter o prazer de apresentar	to have the pleasure of
(alguém)	introducing (someone)

On being introduced, you say **muito prazer**, state your name and shake hands. Women may kiss each other instead of shaking hands.

– **Podes apresentar-me aos teus amigos?**
Will you introduce me to your friends?

– **Tenho o prazer de apresentar um antigo colega de curso.**
I have the pleasure of introducing an old college friend.

– **Muito prazer, António Lopes.**
António Lopes. Pleased to meet you.

– **O prazer é todo meu, Manuela Sá.**
Manuela Sá. Delighted. (The pleasure is all mine.)

– **Ontem fui apresentada ao Director.**
Yesterday I was introduced to the Director.

12.10   FORMS OF ADDRESS[B]

12.10.1   Informal

tu/você[B]	you (sing.)	**vocês**[B,1]	you (pl.)

[1] Although meaning 'you', **você and vocês** are combined with pronouns and verbal forms in the third person. As **vós** (2nd person pl.) has become obsolete in modern Portuguese, **vocês** works as the plural of **tu**.

– **Onde é que vocês vão hoje à noite?**
Where are you going tonight?

– **Vamos ao cinema. Tu também queres vir?**
We are going to the cinema. Do you want to come as well?

12.10.2   Less informal

(verbal third person, subject unstated)[B,1]	you
você	you (sing.)
vocês	you (pl.)

| o + name or surname | you (male being spoken to) |
| a + name[2] | you (female being spoken to) |

[1] Although gaining in popularity, in Portugal **você** is still not widely accepted as a polite form of address. Some people find it patronizing and others can even find it offensive. To address people for whom **tu** is excessively informal, **o senhor** is excessively formal and **você** is unacceptable, it is common practice to use the third person of the required verb, as if one were using **você** but without actually saying it. If the subject needs to be stated, then use the name of the person being spoken to, as if it were a pronoun.

[2] As a rule, women are never addressed by their surname.

- **O Francisco e a Daniela, como estão de visita, não querem vir também?**
  As you are here on a visit, wouldn't you (Francisco and Daniela) like to come too?

- **Nós gostávamos imenso de ver um filme português. O Silva é muito amável em nos convidar. Pode dar-nos boleia para o cinema?**
  We would love to see a Portuguese film. It is very kind of you (Silva) to invite us. Can you give us a lift to the cinema?

12.10.3   Formal[B]

o(s) senhor(es)	you (sir, ladies and gentlemen)
a(s) senhora(s)	you (madam, ladies)
o(s) menino(s)	you (boy, boys and girls), master
a(s) menina(s)	you (girl, girls), miss[B]

Note: These forms can double up as subject pronouns.

- **Os meninos sentem-se aqui enquanto a Menina Fernanda vai comprar os bilhetes para o museu.**
  You (boys and girls) sit here whilst Miss Fernanda is buying the museum tickets.

- **Sra. D. Celeste, posso ir à casa de banho?**
  Mrs (surname) can I go to the toilet?

- **A menina tem que esperar até a Menina Fernanda voltar.**
  You (young girl) must wait until Miss Fernanda returns.

- **As senhoras sabem a que horas termina a visita?**
  Do you (ladies) know at what time the visit ends?

Other ways of saying 'you':

| **V. Exa. (Vossa Excelência)**[B] | you (in writing or very formal occasions) |
| **V. Rev. (Vossa Reverência)** | you (member of the clergy) |

- **V. Exa. pode indicar a entrada para a sala de audiências?**
  Can you (Sir/Madam) show me the way to the reception room?

- **É ao fundo à direita. Na antecâmara V. Rev. deve pedir que o anunciem a Sua Eminência.**
  It is at the end on your right. In the antechamber you (Reverend father) must ask to be announced to His Eminence.

12.10.4   Titles[B]

Sr. + surname	Mr ...
Sra. D. + first name	Mrs ...
Sr(a). + profession, position or title	
Dr./Sr. Dr. + surname	Dr ... (male)
Dra./Sra. Dra. + first name	Dr ... (female)

Note: The full title is used in formal occasions and in writing. In every day communication the initial **Sr.** is dropped and only the professional title is used. As a rule, women's titles are combined with first names whereas men's titles are combined with surnames.

Other titles and formal forms of address:

Sr(a). Eng$^{o(a)}$. ...	for an engineer
Sr(a). Arq$^{to(ta)}$. ...	for an architect
Sr(a). Professor(a) ...	for a teacher
Sr(a). Professor(a) Doutor(a) ...	for a university professor
Sr(a). Ministro(a) (do/da + portfolio)	for a minister
Sr(a). Conde/Condessa (de ...)	for a count/countess
Vossa Excelência (V.Exa.)	government and armed forces officials
Vossa Reverência (V.Rev.)	for members of clergy
Vossa Eminência (V.Ema.)	for a cardinal
Vossa Alteza (V.A.)	for princes and dukes
Vossa Majestade (V.M.)	for kings and emperors
Vossa Santidade (V.S.)	for popes

Note: Whenever these titles and forms of address need to be used as Object Pronouns, they can assume the form of **o senhor** or **Vossa Excelência**, depending on the degree of formality of the occasion. Any titles and forms of address with **Vossa** change into **Sua** when used as third person (see the dialogue in 12.10.3).

- **O Dr. Lemos já chegou?**
  Has Dr Lemos already arrived?

– **Ainda não. O Sr. Engº. deseja deixar recado?**
Not yet. Would you like to leave a message?

– **Não. Prefiro falar com o Arqtº. Sousa Leitão.**
No. I prefer to speak to Mr Sousa Leitão.

– **Também não está. Foi chamado a uma reunião com o Sr. Ministro das Obras Públicas.**
He is not in either. He was called to a meeting with the Minister for Public Works.

12.10.5   Family[B]

o pai, o papá[B]	father, daddy
a mãe, a mamã[B]	mother, mummy
o avô, o vovô[B]	grandfather, grandad
a avó, a vovó[B]	grandmother, grandma
o tio + (first name)	uncle ...
a tia + (first name)	aunt ...

Note: Members of the family belonging to the same generation as the speaker, or younger, are addressed by their first name. In Portugal any member of the family can be addressed informally by **tu** or less informally by their degree of kinship, **o avô, o pai, a mamã**, etc. depending on family habits.

– **A avó tem quem a leve a casa?**
Have you got someone to take you home, grandma?

– **Talvez possa ir com o teu tio Armando e tia Lita.**
Perhaps I could go with your uncle Armando and aunt Lita.

– **Os tios podem levar a avó a casa?**
Can you take grandma home?

– **Podemos. Pergunta aos teus pais se depois querem vir connosco ao café.**
All right. Ask your parents if they would like to come to the café with us later.

– **O pai e a mãe querem ir com os tios ao café, depois de levarem a avó a casa?**
Would you (mum and dad) like to go to the café with uncle Armando and aunt Lita after they have taken grandma home?

Note the different forms of address and of saying 'you' in the above illustrative dialogue.

12.11   TALKING ABOUT ONE'S HEALTH

12.11.1   In small talk and greetings

Q: **Como está(s)?**	How are you?
A: **Bem, obrigado/a.**	Well, thank you.
Menos mal.	So-so.
Óptimo/a!	Very well.
Benzinho.	Fairly well.

In Portuguese you usually answer the question on your health with any of the answers suggested above. One's health is a favourite topic for conversation in Portuguese.

12.11.2   At the surgery/hospital

12.11.2.1   Asking what you feel

Como se sente?	How do you feel?
O que sente?	What do you feel?
Tem ... (dores, febre, nausea, etc.)?	Have you got ... (pain, a temperature, nausea, etc.)?
Sente ... ?	Do you feel ... ?

12.11.2.2   Saying what you feel

Tenho ... (dores, febre, etc.)	I have ... (pain, a temperature)
Sinto ...	I feel ...
Doi-me ... (a cabeça, um dente, etc.)	I have ... (head/tooth-ache)

12.11.2.3   Telling you what to do

Abra a boca.	Open your mouth.
Respire fundo.	Breath deeply.
Deite-se de costas.	Lie on your back.
Deite-se de barriga para baixo.	Lie on your tummy.
Tire o casaco.	Take off your coat/jacket.
Arregace a manga.	Roll up your sleeve.
Tome ... (name of medicine)	Take ...
Deve tomar ...	You should take ...
Tem que tomar ...	You must take ...

... dois comprimidos três vezes ao dia.
... two tablets three times daily.

... uma cápsula quatro vezes ao dia.
... one capsule four times daily.

... uma drageia de seis em seis horas.
... one tablet every six hours.

Note: Doctors' instructions are given with the Present Subjunctive because they are polite commands (see 7.3.1 and 7.4).

12.11.2.4 *Asking what you can/should do*

Posso ... (fazer a minha vida normal, beber, comer de tudo, etc.)?
Can I ... (carry on as normal, drink, eat anything, etc.)?

Devo ... (fazer dieta, repousar, etc.)?
Should I ... (diet, rest)?

Tenho que ... (faltar ao trabalho, etc.)?
Do I have to ... (miss work)?

Tenho que tomar ... (name of medicine)?
Must I take ...

Quantas vezes ao dia?
How many times a day?

12.12   PLACES AND LOCATIONS

12.12.1   Identifying places

Isto é ... (Lisboa, o Algarve, a Madeira)   This is ... (Lisbon, the Algarve, Madeira)

... (place name) fica em ... (place)   ... (place name) ... is in ... (place)

12.12.2   Talking about places

Onde é ... (place)?   Where is ... ?
Onde fica ... (place, building, etc.)?   Where is ... ?

Como é ... (o Minho, Guimarães, etc.)?   What is ... like?
Como são ... (os Açores, as praias, etc.)?   What are the ... like?

– **Onde é Guimarães?**
– Where is Guimarães?

– **É no Minho.**
– It is in Minho.

– **Onde fica o Castelo?**
Where is the castle situated?

- **Fica no centro da cidade.**
In the centre of town.

- **Como é o castelo?**
What is it like?

- **É muito antigo, de muralhas grossas de pedra.**
It is very old with thick stone walls.

- **Como são as ruas?**
What are the streets like?

- **São estreitas, fechadas ao trânsito.**
They are narrow and closed to the traffic.

12.12.3　Talking about place of origin, point of departure

De onde é?　　　　　　　　　Where are you from?
De onde vem?　　　　　　　　Where do you come from?
De onde vem ... (person,　　　Where does ... come from?
product)**?**
É daí que vem ... (person,　　　Does ... come from there?
product)**?**

- **De onde é?**
Where are you from?

- **Sou da Régua.**
I am from Régua.

- **E de onde é a sua colega?**
And where is your colleague from?

- **É da Alijó.**
She is from Alijó.

- **É daí que vem o vinho do Porto?**
Is that where Port comes from?

- **É.**
Yes.

- **E de onde vem o vinho do Dão?**
And where does Dão wine come from?

- **Vem da região de Viseu.**
It comes from the region around Viseu.

12.12.4   Place of residence and addresses

Onde mora?	Where do you live?
Moro ... (place name or address)	I live in ...
Mora em ... (place name, city area)?	Do you live in ... ?
Mora na/o ... (address)?	

Qual é a sua morada?	What is your address?
Qual é a morada do/a ... (person, institution)?	What is the address of ... ?
É na/o ... (address).	It is in ...

Onde vive?	Where do you live?
Vivo em ... (country, region, town).	I live in ...
Onde vive ... (name of person)?	Where does ... live?
Vive em ... (country, region, town).	He/she lives in ...

Note: **Viver** is more general and can refer to the country, region, city or address where one lives. **Morar** is more specific and refers only to the address or town where one lives. If in doubt, use **viver** as you have a greater chance of being correct.

- **Vive em Lisboa?**
  Do you live in Lisbon?

- **Não, vivo no Porto.**
  No, I live in Oporto.

- **Qual é a sua morada?**
  What is your address?

- **Rua dos Loios, 23 – 5° Esq.**
  Rua dos Loios, 23 – 5th floor, left.

- **E os seus pais onde moram?**
  And where do your parents live?

- **Moram em Marco de Canavezes.**
  They live in Marco de Canavezes.

- **Qual é a morada deles?**
  What is their address?

- **Largo do Anjo, 350 – r/c Dt°.**
  Largo do Anjo, 350 – ground floor, right.

12.13   TALKING ABOUT THE WEATHER

Most statements about the weather are made with the verb **estar** because the weather is by its own nature *changeable*. Often the continuous form **estar a ...**[B] is used, as one describes the present weather conditions (see 11.13).

Está bom tempo.	The weather is good.
Está mau tempo.	The weather is bad.
Está calor.	It is hot.
Está frio.	It is cold.
Está sol.	It is sunny.
Está vento.	It is windy.
Está uma aragem.	There is a light breeze.
Está um vento fresco.	There is a coolish wind.
Está a chover.[B]	It is raining.
Está a nevar.[B]	It is snowing.
Está a trovejar.[B]	There is a thunderstorm.
Está a relampejar.[B]	It is lightning.

With the idiom **estar a fazer**[B] it is possible to make a more dynamic description of the weather or even intensify the weather conditions:

Está a fazer sol.[B]	The sun is shining.
Está a fazer vento.[B]	The wind is blowing.
Está a fazer frio.[B]	It is very cold.

The expressions **ardente**, **de derreter**, **de rachar** can further intensify the description of the weather conditions. In the latter cases the preposition **de** introduces a metaphor.

Está um calor de derreter.	It is swelteringly hot.
Está um calor de morrer.	It is stiflingly hot.
Está um frio de rachar.	It is piercingly cold.
Está um frio de morrer.	It is deadly cold.

Any changes in the weather are expressed with the respective verbs which imply a change in temperature:

aquecer	to warm up	arrefecer	to cool down
esfriar	to cool down	refrescar	to cool down

– **Ontem à noite fez muito frio.**
  It was very cold last night.

– **As noites ainda arrefecem muito.**
  It still gets very cold at night.

– **Sim, mas em Abril já era para começarem a aquecer.**
  Yes, but for April they should already be getting warmer.

13 EXCHANGING FACTUAL INFORMATION

13.1 IDENTIFYING PEOPLE

The most helpful structures in this case are those related to 'Interrogative pronouns' (section 5.5, particularly 5.5.2 and 5.5.5).

The verb most used is **ser** ('to be') (see 11.13).

13.1.2 Identity

Quem é?	Who is it?
Quem é ... (someone)?	Who is ... ?
Quem são ... ?	Who are ... ?
Qual é ... (someone)?	Which is ... ?
Quais são ... ?	Which are ... ?
Como é ... (someone)?	What is ... like?

– **Quem é?**
  Who is it?

– **Sou eu, a Ana, podes abir a porta?**
  It's me, Ana, can you open the door?

– **Quem são as pessoas que acabam de sair?**
  Who are the people who have just left?

– **São os vizinhos do quarto andar.**
  They are my fourth-floor neighbours.

– **Qual é a filha mais nova?**
  Which is their youngest daughter?

– **É a de casaco vermelho.**
  The one in the red jacket.

– **Quais são os mais simpáticos?**
  Which are the nicest?

– **São os do quinto andar.**
  The ones on the fifth floor.

– **E como são os vizinhos do lado?**
  And what are the next-door neighbours like?

– **Não sei, estão sempre fora.**
  I don't know; they are always away.

13.1.3 Ownership

De quem é ... (something)?	Whose ... is this/that?
Que ... (something) **é este/esta?**	Whose ... is this/that?

A quem pertence ... (something)?	Whom does ... belong to?

É/são ... (possessive).	It/they is/are ...
É/são de ... (someone).	It/they belong(s) to ...

- **De quem é esta carteira?**
  Whose handbag is this?

- **É da Ana Isabel.**
  It belongs to Ana Isabel.

- **E que óculos são estes?**
  And what about the glasses?

- **Também são dela.**
  They are also hers.

- **E as luvas, a quem pertencem?**
  And the gloves, whose are they?

- **São do Rui. Esqueceu-as aqui. Mas as luvas vermelhas são minhas.**
  They are Rui's. He left them behind. But the red ones are mine.

13.1.4 Profession, occupation

Que é ... (someone)?	
O que é ...?	
Que faz ...?	What does ... do?
O que faz ...?	

Qual é a tua/sua profissão?	What is your profession?
Qual é a profissão de ... (someone)?	What is ... profession?
Qual é o posto de ... (someone)?	What is ... rank?

Onde trabalha/s?	Where do you work?
	Who do you work for?

Onde trabalha ... (someone)?	Where does ... work?
	Who does ... work for?

Trabalho em ... (somewhere).	I work in ...
Em que firma trabalha?	Who do you work for?
Trabalho na ... (firm name).	I work for ...
Estou na ... (firm name/service).	I work for ...

- **Que é o teu primo?**
  What does your cousin do?

- **É contabilista.**
  He is an accountant.

- **E onde é que ele trabalha?**
  And where does he work?

- **Trabalha num hotel. E o teu irmão?**
  In a hotel. And your brother?

- **O meu irmão está na Marinha.**
  He is in the Navy.

- **Qual é o posto dele?**
  What is his rank?

- **É primeiro tenente.**
  He is a lieutenant.

- **O teu pai também é da Marinha?**
  Is your father also in the Navy?

- **Não, já está reformado.**
  No, he is already retired.

13.2 IDENTIFYING THINGS

O que é isto/aquilo?	What is this/that?
Que ... (something) **é este/a?**	What ... is this?
Que tipo/espécie de (something) **é/são?**	What kind of ... is/are ... ?
Como é ... (something)**?**	What is ... like?
De que é?	What is it made of?
De que é feito?	What is it made out of?
Como é feito?	How is it made?
Como se faz?	How does one make it?

- **O que é isto?**
  What is this?

- **É uma torta.**
  It is a tart.

- **De que é?**
  What is it made of?

- **É de amêndoa.**
It is an almond tart.

- **Como é feita?**
How does one make it?

- **No forno, com um recheio de ovos e amêndoa.**
In the oven with an egg and almond filling.

- **E que doce é este?**
And what dessert is this?

- **São farófias.**
They are 'farófias'.

- **Como são as farófias?**
What are they like?

- **São claras batidas cozidas em leite e com molho de ovos.**
They are beaten egg whites boiled in milk, with an egg sauce.

13.3 ASKING FOR INFORMATION[B]

Pode-me dizer[B] ... (sentence with interrogative)?   Could you tell me ... ?

Importa-se de me dizer ... ?   Would you mind telling me ... ?

Diga-me[B] ... (sentence with interrogative), **por favor.**   Can you please tell me ... ?

Sabe dizer-me[B] ... (sentence with interrogative)?   Could you tell me ... ?

Note: These phrases usually introduce a question with an interrogative pronoun (see section 5.5), an adverb (see 8.1(i)) or a conjunction (see section 9.2.8).

- **Pode-me dizer qual é a estrada para Espinho?**
Can you tell me which is the road to Espinho?

- **É a primeira à direita.**
It is the first on the right.

- **Diga-me se há próximo uma bomba de gasolina, por favor.**
Could you please tell me whether there is a petrol station near by?

- **Há uma à saída da cidade.**
There is one as you leave town.

- **E sabe dizer-me se está aberta a esta hora?**
Do you know whether it is still open?

– **Está aberta até às dez da noite.**
It is open until 10 p.m.

– **Importa-se de me dizer as horas?**
Can you tell me the time?

– **São dez para as dez.**
It is 9.50.

13.3.1   Asking the time

Que horas são?	What time is it?
Tem horas?	Have you got the time?
Sabe-me dizer as horas?	Can you tell me the time?
A que horas ... ?	At what time ... ?

13.3.2   Telling the time

É/são ...	It is ...
Meio-dia	noon, midday
Meia-noite	midnight
... (hour) e um quarto	a quarter past ...
... (hour) menos um quarto	a quarter to ...
um quarto para a(s) ...	a quarter to ...
... (hour) e meia	half past ...
... (hour) e ... (minutes)	(used with schedules and timetables)
às ...	at ...
das ... às ...	from ... to ...
da manhã/da tarde	a.m./p.m.

– **Tens horas?**
Have you got the time?

– **São onze e um quarto.**
It is a quarter past eleven.

– **A que horas chega o comboio da Ana?**
At what time does Ana's train arrive?

– **Chega às 13 e 55.**
At 13.55.

– **Podes ir buscá-la à estação? Tenho uma aula às duas da tarde.**
Can you meet her at the station? I have a class at 2 p.m.

– **Está bem. Sendo assim, podemos sair de casa por volta do meio-dia
  e meia, deixo-te na faculdade à uma e sigo depois para a estação.**
  All right. In that case, we can leave the house at about half past
  twelve, I can leave you at the university at one and then I'll make
  my way to the station.

13.4 REPORTING, DESCRIBING AND NARRATING

(a) These are all interrelated language functions. The main requirement
to perform these functions correctly is to have a good knowledge of
verbs, their tenses and the meaning of each tense (see Chapter 7).
The Present (7.2.1), Imperfect (7.2.3) and Preterite (7.2.4) tenses are
particularly important.

(b) Do not forget that when narrating an event which took place in the
past, the Imperfect refers to the background state or action whereas
the Preterite refers to the incident which occurs *once* at a given
moment, frequently against the background described by the
Imperfect (see 7.2.3.1d and 7.2.4.1b).

(c) The Imperfect can also imply the idea of habit or repetition (7.2.3.1b).

(d) The Present Perfect in Portuguese, contrary to most other languages,
is a continuous tense. It describes an action that began in the past,
has been developing until now and may even continue into the future
(7.2.2.1a). It is a very fluid tense – no set start to the action and no
set end.

(e) A good knowledge of nouns, adjectives, pronouns, their inflections,
prepositions, conjunctions, etc. is also required.

(f) There are no set formulas for these functions, as each sentence will
depend on what you have to say.
   The best advice is always to *try and think in Portuguese*, using as
many set phrases, formulas and structures as you have learnt so far,
and adapting them to the message you have to communicate. This is
particularly important if you are a beginner. Avoid at all costs thinking
in your mother tongue and then translating into Portuguese.
   If you compare the examples we give you in each section and the
respective translation, you will notice that you are seldom presented
with literal translations. That is because literal translations seldom
work.

Quando eu era pequena íamos sempre passar o Verão a Mira. Tínhamos lá uma casa junto à praia onde havia uma lagoa enorme e as crianças podiam brincar e nadar em segurança.

Um dia, de repente, levantou-se um grande temporal. Uma onda gigantesca varreu a praia e chegou a fazer transbordar a lagoa. O meu irmão mais novo quase morreu afogado. Os meus pais, preocupados, nunca mais nos deram a mesma liberdade ao brincar na praia e passámos a fazer férias no campo.

Ultimamente, esses tempos da minha infância têm-me vindo à memória e espero, em breve, voltar a Mira ... com os meus filhos.

When I was young we used to spend the Summer in Mira. We had a house there, near the beach, where there was a huge lagoon and the children could swim and play in safety.

One day, suddenly, there was a big storm. A huge wave swept the beach and caused the lagoon to overflow. My younger brother nearly drowned. My parents, who were worried, never gave us the same freedom when playing on the beach and we began spending our holidays in the countryside.

Lately, those days of my youth have been coming back to me and I hope, soon, to return to Mira ... with my children.

13.4.1 Reporting

The advice given above applies equally to reporting in general, but a few guidelines are useful when reproducing and reporting speech.

Avoid repeating the same verb to introduce consecutive items of speech. Use different verbs, but make sure that they reflect the nature of the speech they refer to. Here is a useful list:

dizer	to say	**informar**	to inform
declarar	to state, to declare	**afirmar**	to state
assegurar	to assure	**garantir**	to guarantee
insistir	to insist		
acrescentar	to add	**comentar**	to comment
criticar	to criticize		
perguntar	to ask	**interrogar**	to query
inquirir	to inquire	**indagar**	to sound out

– **Eu não roubei o carro!, declarou o ladrão. Mas o polícia comentou duvidoso:**

'I didn't steal the car!', declared the thief. But the policeman commented doubtfully:

– **Isso é o que se vai ver!, e acrescentou à queima-roupa: – É por isso que as chaves estavam no bolso do teu casaco.**
'That remains to be seen!', and he added as an aside: 'That's why the keys were in the pocket of your jacket.'

– **Mas esse casaco não é o meu!, assegurou o ladrão. – É tudo uma tramoia para me incriminar – afirmou.**
'But that jacket is not mine!', assured the thief. 'This is all a plot to frame me', he stated.

– **Ontem estive todo o dia no trabalho – insistiu ele.**
'Yesterday I was at work all day', he insisted.

Note: There is inversion of subject and verb when the direct speech is presented first and the reference to the speaker comes after.

13.4.1.1 *Direct speech/Reported speech*

In reported speech the same range of introductory verbs is used as in direct speech, but the sequence of verbal tenses is different. A different sequence of adverbs of place and time, possessives and demonstratives is also required:

	Direct speech	*Reported speech*
verbs	Present	Imperfect
	Present Perfect, Preterite	Past Perfect
	Present and Future Subjunctive	Past Subjunctive
	Present Perfect Subjunctive	Past Perfect Subjunctive
adverbs of place	**aqui**	**ali**
	cá	**lá**
adverbs of time	**ontem**	**no dia anterior**
	hoje	**nesse/naquele dia**
	amanhã	**no dia seguinte**
possessives	first and second person	third person
demonstratives	**isto**	**isso, aquilo**
	este/esse	**aquele**
	estes/esses	**aqueles**

Now look at the new version of the previous dialogue in reported speech:

O ladrão declarou que não tinha roubado o carro. Mas o polícia comentou duvidoso que isso era o que se ia ver, e acrescentou, à queima-roupa, que era por isso que as chaves estavam no bolso do casaco dele. O ladrão, no entanto, assegurou que aquele não era o seu casaco, afirmou que era tudo uma tramoia para o incriminar e insistiu que no dia anterior tinha estado todo o tempo no trabalho.

The thief declared that he had not stolen the car. But the policeman added doubtfully, as an aside, that that was the reason why the keys had been left in the pocket of the thief's jacket. The thief, however, assured him that the jacket in question was not his, stated that it was all a plot to frame him and insisted that the day before he had been at work all the time.

13.5 LETTER WRITING

Letter writing is also related to reporting, narrating and describing, but letters contain specific elements such as a record of the date, typical opening and closing formulas, and the text itself often makes ample use of the Subjunctive, as letters often contain good wishes, requests or even commands.

13.5.1 Dates[B]

- Always on the top right-hand side of the page.
- Write the place, the day in cardinal numbers, the month and the year.

Porto, 30 de Novembro[B] de 1998   Oporto, 30 November 1998

13.5.2 Opening Formulas

13.5.2.1 Formal

Exmo(a). Senhor(a)[B]   Dear Sir/Madam
Exmo(a). Sr. + (profession, position, title + surname)   Dear Mr/Dr/Captain/etc. . . .

13.5.2.2 Less formal

(**Meu/Minha**) **caro(a)** + (name)   Dear . . .
(**Meu/Minha**) **caro(a) amigo(a)**   Dear friend
(**Meu/Minha**) **caro(a) colega**   Dear colleague

13.5.2.3 Informal

Olá + name   Hi . . .

13.5.2.4 Intimate

(Meu/Minha) querido(a) + (name, pai, mãe, tio, irmão ...)	Dear ... father/mother/uncle/ brother/etc.
Meu amor	Dearest

13.5.3 Closing formulas

13.5.3.1 Formal

De V.Exa. muito atentamente	Yours sincerely
Melhores cumprimentos[1]	Yours faithfully

[1] Nowadays, the formula **Melhores cumprimentos** is more widely used.

Santarém, 1 de Março de 1998   Santarém, 1 March 1998

Exmo. Senhor,   Dear Sir,

Agradecemos a V. carta de 25.2.98 e informamos que o pagamento já foi feito no dia 23 do corrente. Agradecíamos que nos enviassem o respectivo recibo.

We thank you for your letter of 25.2.98, and inform you that payment has been made on 23rd of this month. We would be grateful if you could send us the respective receipt.

De V. Exa. muito atentamente, (assinatura)

Yours sincerely, (signature)

13.5.3.2 Less formal

Cumprimentos	Regards	**Um abraço**	Best wishes

13.5.3.3 Informal

Um beijo[1]	Kisses	**Um abraço**	Hugs

[1] **Um beijo** is used between women, from women to men and vice versa, but never between men.

13.5.3.4 Intimate

Um beijo	Love	**Um abraço**	Love
Muitas saudades	Lots of love		

Recife, 3.4.99	Recife, 3.4.99
Cara Guida,	Dear Guida,
Adoro o Recife. O tempo está maravilhoso e as pessoas são fantásticas. Até breve.	I love Recife. The weather is fantastic and the people are wonderful. See you soon.
Saudades,	Love,
(nome)	(name)

13.6 CORRECTING ASSUMPTIONS

The easiest and most straightforward way of correcting assumptions made by someone addressing the speaker is to say **Não** and then confirm the negative with a short negative sentence. A simple '**não**' for an answer is judged somewhat curt and impolite.

Não, não + verb   No, I don't/haven't.

– **Tem troco de 1.000$00?**
Have you got change for Esc. 1,000?

– **Não, não tenho.**
No, I haven't.

Alternatively, one can say **não** and then follow it with a correcting statement. This can be introduced by **mas**, 'but', include the expression **é que**, a confirmation with the verb **ser** or even use a prepositional pronoun to emphasize the correction.

– **O senhor tem troco de 5.000$00?**
Have you got change for Esc. 5,000?

– **Não, só tenho de 1.000$00.**
No, only for Esc. 1,000.

– **Mas nós avisámos que os pagamentos deviam ser feitos no montante exacto.**
But we made it clear that all payments had to be made in the correct amount.

– **Não, a mim niguém disse nada. O senhor falou foi com esta senhora ao lado.**
No, I was not told anything of the sort. The person you spoke to was this lady next to me.

13.6.1　Polite formulas to introduce corrections

Desculpe, mas . . .	Excuse me, but . . .
Lamento, mas . . .	I am sorry, but . . .
Está enganado/a, . . .	You are mistaken, . . .
Está errado/a . . .	You are wrong . . .
Isso não é assim.	That is not so.
Isso não é bem assim.	That is not quite so.

– **Lamento, mas essa promoção já terminou.**
I am sorry, but that special offer has already ended.

– **Desculpe, mas o vale ainda está dentro do prazo.**
Excuse me, but the voucher is still within the expiry date.

– **Está enganado, essa oferta já expirou.**
You are mistaken, that offer has ended.

– **Como pode ser, se as instruções dizem o contrário?**
How is that possible, if the instructions say the opposite?

– **Isso não é bem assim, a oferta só dura enquanto houver stock[1].**
That is not quite so. The offer is only valid as long as stocks last.

---

[1] **Estoque** in Brazilian Portuguese.

14 GETTING THINGS DONE

14.1 SUGGESTING A COURSE OF ACTION

Vamos!	Let's go!
Vamos + (Infinitive phrase)	Let us ...
E se + (phrase with Past Subjunctive)	What if we ...
Porque não + (phrase with Present tense)	Why don't we ...
Podíamos + (Infinitive phrase)	We could ...
Devíamos + (Infinitive phrase)	We should ...

- **E se fôssemos fazer um piquenique?**
  What if we had a picnic?

- **Óptima ideia! Vamos!**
  Great idea! Let's!

- **Podíamos convidar os nossos colegas ingleses.**
  We could invite the English students.

- **Claro, mas devíamos também convidar os outros colegas estrangeiros, porque é uma excelente oportunidade de confraternizar com todos.**
  Of course, but we should also invite the other foreign students, as it is an excellent opportunity to socialize with everybody.

- **Porque não aproveitamos já o próximo fim-de-semana?**
  Why don't we take advantage of next weekend?

14.2 OFFERING TO DO SOMETHING

Quer/queres/querem que[1] + (phrase with Present Subjunctive)**?**	Do you want me to ... ?
Deseja que[1] + (phrase with Present Subjunctive)**?**	Would you like me to ... ?
Posso + (verb in Infinitive)**?**	Can I/May I ... ?
Podemos + (verb in Infinitive)**?**	Can we/May we ...

[1] The Subjunctive must be used with these phrases because they imply an indirect command.

- **Posso ajudar? Querem que traga uns pasteis de bacalhau?**
  Can I help? Do you want me to bring some fish cakes?

- **Nós também podemos dar uma ajuda e trazer uma sobremesa.**
  We can also give you a hand and bring a dessert.

14.3 REQUESTING OTHERS TO DO SOMETHING

Most requests are made with the verb either in the Imperative or in the Present Subjunctive (see sections 7.3 and 7.4), but they can also be introduced by some set formulas followed by phrases with the verb in the Present Subjunctive:

Desejo/desejamos que ...	I/we wish you to ...
Peço/pedimos que ...	I/we ask you to ...
Quero/queremos que ...	I/we want you to ...
Ordeno/ordenamos que ...	I/we order you to ...
Importa-se de + (phrase with Infinitive)?	Would you mind ... ?

Note: All these requests can be either preceded or followed by **por favor**, **se faz favor**, etc.

- **Ó Ana, faz uma torta de amêndoa e traz guardanapos de papel, se fazes favor.**
  Ana, please bake an almond tart and bring paper napkins.

- **Está bem, mas quero que me digas quantas pessoas vais convidar para o piquenique.**
  All right, but I want you to tell me how many people you are inviting to the picnic.

- **Importas-te de me telefonar amanhã à noite? Nessa altura já te posso dizer.**
  Do you mind phoning me tomorrow evening? I can tell you then.

14.4 INVITING OTHERS TO DO SOMETHING

Gostava/s de + (phrase with Infinitive)?	Would you like to ... ?
Quer/es + (phrase with Infinitive)?	Do you want to ... ?
convidar ...	to invite
Está/s convidado/a.	You are invited.
Está/s convidado/a para ...	You are invited to ...

- **O David também quer vir connosco?**[B]
  David, do you want to come too?

- **Claro que quero.**
  Of course I do.

- **Então está convidado.**
  Then you are invited.

- **Também posso convidar a minha irmã?**
  Can I also invite my sister?

- **Com todo o gosto.**
  With pleasure.

- **Então aceito já em nome dela.**
  Then I accept on her behalf.

14.5 ASKING FOR ADVICE; ADVISING OTHERS FOR OR AGAINST SOMETHING

Que aconselha?	What do you advise?
Qual é o teu/seu conselho?	What is your advice?
Que acha(s) que devo fazer?	What do you think I should do?
Aconselho-o/a a + (phrase with Infinitive)	I advise you to . . .
O meu conselho é que + (phrase with Subjunctive)	My advice is that you . . .
Não o/a aconselho a + (phrase with Infinitive)	I advise you not to . . .
Aconselho-o/a a não + (phrase with Infinitive)	I advise you not to . . .
O meu conselho é que não + (phrase with Subjunctive)	My advice is that you should not . . .
No teu/seu lugar + (phrase with Conditional or Imperfect)	If I were you . . .

Note: Some of the expressions above require a Subjunctive because they are equivalent to indirect commands or wishes (see section 7.3).

- **Eu adorava ir ao piquenique, David, mas tenho tanto trabalho para acabar. Que achas que devo fazer?**
  I would love to go to the picnic, David, but I have so much work to finish. What do you think I should do?

- **O meu conselho é que te divirtas primeiro e depois te lances ao trabalho.**
  My advice is that you have some fun first and then you throw yourself into your work.

– **Mas como vou conseguir terminar tudo?**
But how am I going to finish everything?

– **Primeiro aconselho-te a não ficar excessivamente preocupada, e depois é de facto melhor descansar um pouco. No teu lugar, eu não perdia o piquenique.**
First, I advise you not to get too worried and then it is in fact better for you to have a bit of a break. If I were you, I would not miss the picnic.

14.6 WARNING OTHERS

(See also 12.4.2.)

Atenção!	Watch out!
Preste atenção!	Watch out!
Cuidado!	Take care! Watch out!
Perigo!	Danger!
Olha/olhe que ...	Beware/Be careful ...
Tem/tenha cuidado com/porque ...	Be careful because ...
Toma/tome cautela com/porque ...	Beware/Be careful ...
Está avisado/a.	You have been warned/told.

Quiet words of warning can also be expressed by means of sentences with the verb in the Subjunctive. Such sentences are equivalent to indirect or polite commands or wishes (see 7.3).

– **Olhe que é muito perigoso ir nadar com a bandeira vermelha.**
Be careful, because it is dangerous to swim when the red flag is up.

– **Acha que sim? Pensei que aqui não havia perigo.**
Do you think so? I thought there was no danger here.

– **Tome cautela, porque o mar aqui é muito forte e a corrente puxa para longe.**
Be careful, because the sea here is very strong and the current drags you away.

– **Mas eu gosto tanto de nadar.**
But I enjoy swimming so much.

– **Está avisado. Depois não se queixe.**
You have been told. Do not complain later.

14.7 INSTRUCTING OTHERS TO DO/NOT TO DO SOMETHING

These instructions are given using sentences with the verb in the Present Subjunctive because these are, in effect, commands. This type of sentence is used in instructions on how to operate equipment, in cooking recipes, advertising, propaganda, etc. (See 12.11.2.3; doctors' instructions are also given in the Subjunctive.)

Arroz doce

Rice pudding

Ponha uma chávena de arroz numa panela e cubra-o de água. Não deixe ferver mais de 10 minutos. Adicione casca de limão, e sal e, agora, deixe aferventar mais 5 a 10 minutos adicionando leite quente. Quando o arroz estiver cozido, adicione um pouco mais de açúcar do que a quantidade de arroz e deixe ferver um pouco mais. Finalmente, junte duas colheres de sopa de manteiga, mexa até derreter, retire do lume, e sirva numa travessa ou numa taça. Polvilhe com canela.

Put a cupful of rice in a pan and cover it with water. Do not allow it to boil for more than ten minutes. Add lemon rind and salt and now allow to simmer another 5 to 10 minutes, adding hot milk. When the rice is soft, add a little more sugar than the amount of rice used and allow to simmer a little longer. Finally, stir in two dessertspoons of butter, remove from the heat, and pour into a server or a bowl. Sprinkle with cinnamon.

14.8   REQUESTING ASSISTANCE

Once again, as most of these sentences are equivalent to commands or polite requests they require the use of the Subjunctive:

Ajuda/e-me[B] a + (phrase with Infinitive)	Help me to ...
Pode(s) ajudar-me[B] a + (phrase with Infinitive)	Would you help me to ...

Pode(s) dar uma ajuda?	Can you help?
Dá/dê-me[B] **uma ajuda.**	Give me a hand.

– **Ajuda-me a lavar o carro, por favor.**
 Help me wash the car, please.

– **Está bem, mas depois também me dás uma ajuda com o jardim.**
 All right, but afterwards you give me a hand in the garden too.

14.9   STATING WHETHER SOMETHING IS COMPULSORY AND FINDING OUT WHETHER ONE IS OBLIGED OR NOT TO DO SOMETHING

É obrigatório + (phrase with Infinitive)	It is compulsory to ...
Tem que se + (phrase with Infinitive)	One has to ...
Não é obrigatório + (phrase with Infinitive)	It is not compulsory to ...
Não é necessário + (phrase with Infinitive)	It is not necessary to ...

É obrigatório?	Is it compulsory?
Tem que se + (phrase with Infinitive)**?**	Has one got to ... ?
Tenho/temos que + (phrase with Infinitive)**?**	Do I/we have to ... ?

- **É necessário responder ao convite?**
  Do we have to reply to the invitation?

- **Sim, até ao dia 15 deste mês.**
  Yes, up until the 15th of the month.

- **Temos que ir de gravata?**
  Do we have to wear a tie?

- **Não é obrigatório, mas era melhor.**
  It is not compulsory, but it would be advisable.

14.10   SEEKING, GIVING, REFUSING PERMISSION

Pode-se + (phrase with Infinitive)**?**	Can one ... ?
Posso/podemos + (phrase with Infinitive)**?**	May I/we ... ?
É permitido + (phrase with Infinitive)**?**	Is one allowed to ... ?
Temos autorização de/para + (phrase with Infinitive)**?**	Have we permission to ... ?
É possível + (phrase with Infinitive)**?**	Is it possible/Is one allowed to ... ?
É proibido + (phrase with Infinitive)	It is forbidden to ...
Não é permitido + (phrase with Infinitive)	One is not allowed to ...
Dar autorização de/para + (phrase with Infinitive)	Give permission to ...

- **Pode-se fumar?**
  Is smoking allowed?

- **Não. Aqui no refeitório é proibido. mas na sala de convívio já é permitido.**
  No, here in the refectory, it is forbidden, but it is allowed in the Common Room.

- **É possível convidar uma colega inglesa para vir almoçar aqui?**
  Is it possible for me to invite an English colleague for lunch here?

- **Tens que pedir ao director se dá autorização.**
  You must ask the director for permission.

14.11   EXPRESSING AND FINDING OUT ABOUT NEED

Preciso de + (phrase with Infinitive)	I need to ...
Preciso que + (phrase with Subjunctive)	I need to ...

Tenho necessidade de + (phrase with   I need . . .
Infinitive)
Precisa(s) de + (phrase with Infinitive)?   Do you need to . . . ?
Precisa(s) que + (phrase with   Do you need to . . . ?
Subjunctive)?
Tens/Tem necessidade de + (phrase with Do you need . . . ?
Infinitive)?

– **Precisas de dinheiro?**
Do you need any money?

– **Neste momento não, mas amanhã tenho necessidade de ir ao banco
porque preciso de pagar as propinas.**
Not at the moment, but tomorrow I have to go to the bank because
I need to pay my fees.

14.12 ENQUIRING AND EXPRESSING INTENTION, WANT OR DESIRE

Tenciona(s) + (phrase with Infinitive)?   Do you intend to . . . ?
Que tenciona(s) + (Infinitive)?   What do you intend to . . . ?
Tens/Tem a intenção de + (phrase   Do you intend to . . . ?
with Infinitive)?
Está(s) decidido/a a + (phrase with   Have you decided to . . . ?
Infinitive)?
Deseja(s) + (phrase with Infinitive)?   Do you wish to . . . ?
Quer(es) + (phrase with Infinitive)?   Do you want to . . . ?
Quero + (phrase with Infinitive)   I want to . . .
Tenho a intenção de + (phrase   I intend to . . .
with Infinitive)
Faço tenção/tenções de + (phrase with   I intend to . . .
Infinitive)

– **Que tencionas fazer quando terminares o curso?**
What do you intend to do when you finish your degree?

– **Quero ir trabalhar em Angola.**
I want to work in Angola.

– **Estás mesmo decidido a sair de Portugal?**
Are you quite decided to leave Portugal?

– **Estou. Só faço tenções de regressar ao fim de dois anos.**
Yes, I am. I only intend to return at the end of two years.

15 FINDING OUT AND EXPRESSING INTELLECTUAL ATTITUDES

15.1 ENQUIRING ABOUT AND EXPRESSING AGREEMENT AND DISAGREEMENT

Que acha(s)?	What do you think?
Acha(s) que sim?	Do you accept/approve? Do you think so?
Acha(s) bem?	Do you think it is all right?
Concorda(s)?	Do you agree?
Está(s) de acordo?	Do you agree?
Não acha(s) bem?	Don't you agree/approve?
Não concorda(s)?	Don't you agree? You do not agree?
Não está(s) de acordo?	Don't you agree? You do not agree?
Acha(s) que não?[1]	You do not approve?
Tem/tens objecções?[1]	Do you object?
Não tem/tens objecções?[1]	Don't you object?
Quais são as objecções?	What have you got against it?

Está bem.	All right.
Acho bem.	I agree.
Muito bem.	Very well. Very good.
Boa ideia!	Good idea!
Concordo.	I agree.
Concordo plenamente!	I completely agree.
Penso/acho que sim.	I think so.

Não senhor!	Absolutely not!
Não concordo.	I do not agree.
Discordo.	I disagree.
Discordo plenamente!	I thoroughly disagree!
Penso/acho que não.	I don't think so.

Não pode ser!	That is not possible.
Nem pensar!	Heaven forbid!
Redondamente não!	Absolutely not!

Não se pode tolerar que + (phrase with Subjunctive)   It cannot be tolerated that ...

---

[1] These questions are half expecting an expression of disagreement.

- **No Verão podíamos ir numa excursão ao Amazonas. Que achas?**
  In the Summer we could go on a trip to the Amazon. What do you think?

– **Eu acho bem. É uma óptima ideia.**
I agree. It is a fantastic idea.

– **Pois eu acho que não.**
Well, I disagree.

– **Não achas bem ir visitar uma das regiões mais fascinantes do mundo, e que está em risco de extinção?**
Don't you approve of visiting one of the most fascinating regions in the world, which is in danger of extinction?

– **Eu, não. Discordo plenamente.**
No, I don't! I thoroughly disagree.

– **Quais são as objecções?**
What have you got against it?

– **Não se pode tolerar que turistas como nós contribuam para danificar ainda mais o ambiente. Além disso, íamos estragar as férias a palmilhar a selva por um calor insuportável. Nem pensar!**
It is intolerable that tourists like us contribute towards further damaging the environment. Besides, our holidays would be spoilt, trotting about the jungle in unbearable heat. Heaven forbid!

15.2 ENQUIRING AND STATING WHETHER YOU KNOW SOMETHING OR SOMEONE

O que é isto?	What is this?
Sabe(s) o que é isto?	Do you know what this is?
Conhece(s) este produto?	Do you know this product?
Sabe(s) se . . . ?	Do you know if . . . ?
Sabe(s) dizer-me se . . . ?	Can you tell me if . . . ?
Conhece(s) . . . (someone)?	Do you know/Are you acquainted with . . . ?
Conhece(s) bem . . . ?	Are you well acquainted with . . . ?
Sei, sim. **Conheço, sim.** }	Yes, I do (know something).
Conheço bem . . .	I am well acquainted with . . .
Conheço mal . . .	I do not know (someone/something) very well. / I am not well acquainted with . . .
Não sei . . .	I do not know (something).
Não conheço . . .	I do not know (someone).
Desconheço . . .	I do not know (something/someone).
Desconheço por completo.	I really do not know.
Não sei de todo.	I do not know at all.

- **Sabe quem é o Dr. Sampaio?**
  Do you know Dr Sampaio?

- **Sei, sim. É médico de clínica geral neste centro clínico.**
  Yes, I do. He is a GP in this surgery.

- **Sabe dizer-me se já chegou?**
  Can you tell me whether he has already arrived?

- **O Dr. Sampaio já veio e já saiu. Às terças-feiras só dá consulta de manhã.**
  Dr. Sampaio has been and has already left. He only sees patients in the morning on Tuesdays.

- **Sabe se deixou recado para mim? Tinha-me dito que viesse falar sobre os resultados das análises.**
  Do you know whether he left a message for me? He told me to come and discuss the result of my tests.

- **Desconheço completamente. O Dr. Sampaio não está e não deixou qualquer recado.**
  I really do not know. Dr Sampaio is not in and he has left no message.

15.3 ENQUIRING AND STATING WHETHER YOU REMEMBER SOMETHING OR SOMEONE

Lembras-te de ... ?	
Lembra-se de ... ?	Do you remember ... ?
Não te lembras/recordas de ... ?	
Não se lembra/recorda de ... ?	Don't you remember ... ?
Esqueceste-te de ... ?	
Esqueceu-se de ... ?	Have you forgotten ... ?
Sim, lembro.	Yes, I remember.
Lembro-me bem de ...	I remember ... well.
Não me lembro.	I do not remember.
Não me lembro nada.	I do not remember at all.
Não me lembro de nada.	I do not/cannot remember a thing.
Tenho uma ideia.	I have an idea.
Tenho uma vaga ideia.	I have a vague idea.
Não tenho ideia nenhuma.[1]	I have no idea.
Não faço a mínima ideia.	I haven't got the faintest idea.

[1] If you change the word order into **Não tenho nenhuma ideia**, it means 'I do not have any ideas'.

– **Recorda-se de eu ter vindo aqui ontem fazer compras?**
Do you remember me coming here yesterday to do some shopping?

– **Sim, recordo bem.**
Yes, I remember it well.

– **É que paguei 5.500$00 na caixa por dois CDs, mas esqueci-me de os levantar. Lembra-se?**
I paid Esc. 5,500 at the till for a couple of CDs, but I forgot to take them with me. Do you remember?

– **Não. Não faço a mínima ideia.**
No. I haven't the faintest idea.

– **Tente recordar-se. Eu vim com uma amiga directamente do trabalho. Estávamos as duas com o uniforme da polícia.**
Try to remember. I came directly from work with a friend. We were both wearing our police uniform.

– **Ah! Sim, pareço recordar-me agora.**
Oh! Yes, I seem to remember now.

15.4 FINDING OUT AND STATING WHETHER SOMETHING IS POSSIBLE OR IMPOSSIBLE

This type of sentence requires two basic phrase structures with the main verb in either the Infinitive or the Subjunctive:

Infinitive: when you want to ask or to state whether it is possible or impossible to do something, e.g. **É impossível eles chegarem a horas**.

Subjunctive: when you want to judge whether something is possible or impossible. As this is the same as putting forward a hypothesis, a Subjunctive is required (see 7.3c): e.g. **É impossível que eles cheguem a horas**.

É possível?	Is it possible?
É possível + (phrase with Infinitive)?	Is it possible to ... ?
É possível que[1] + (phrase with Subjunctive)?	Is it possible to/that ... ?
Será possível + (phrase with Infinitive)?	Will it be possible?
Será possível que[1] + (phrase with Subjunctive)?	Can it be possible ... ?
Não é possível?	Is it not possible?
É impossível?	Is it impossible?
É impossível + (phrase with Infinitive)?	Is it impossible to ... ?

É impossível que[1] + (phrase with Subjunctive)**?**	Is it not possible ... ?
Talvez.	Perhaps/Maybe.
Talvez + (phrase with Subjunctive)	Perhaps/Maybe ...
Talvez sim/não.	Probably yes/not.
Provavelmente.	Probably.
Provavelmente + (phrase with Indicative)	Probably ...
É provável que + (phrase with Subjunctive)	It is likely that ...
É muito provável que + (phrase with Subjunctive)	It is very likely that ...
É pouco provável que + (phrase with Subjunctive)	It is unlikely that ...
É muito pouco provável que + (phrase with Subjunctive)	It is highly unlikely that ...
É possível.	It is possible.
É possível + (phrase with Infinitive)	It is possible to ...
É possível que + (phrase with Subjunctive)	It is possible that ...
É impossível.	It is impossible.
É impossível + (phrase with Infinitive)	It is impossible to ...
É impossível que + (phrase with Subjunctive)	It is impossible that ...
Não pode ser!	It can't be possible!
Não é possível que + (phrase with Subjunctive)	It can't be possible that ...

[1] These phrases can imply disbelief.

- **É possível marcar uma passagem para Londres no voo de amanhã de manhã?**
  Is it possible to make a booking for tomorrow morning's flight to London?

- **No voo da manhã é impossível, está esgotado, mas no da tarde talvez, embora seja pouco provável nesta época do ano.**
  On the morning flight it's not possible; it is fully booked. Perhaps on the afternoon flight, although it is unlikely at this time of the year.

- **Veja lá. Tenho que estar em Londres na quinta-feira.**
  See what you can do. I have to be in London by Thursday.

- **Lamento, mas, afinal, também não é possível. Só quinta-feira de manhã.**
  I am sorry but it is not possible either. Only Thursday morning.

– **Não pode ser! Será possível que com tantos voos diários, não me
consegue arranjar nada antes de quinta-feira?**
It can't be! How can it be possible that with so many daily flights,
you cannot find me anything before Thursday?

– **Lamento muito, mas é de todo impossível arranjar um voo mais cedo.**
I am very sorry, but it is absolutely impossible to find a flight any
earlier.

15.5 FINDING OUT AND STATING WHETHER SOMETHING IS CONSIDERED A LOGICAL CONCLUSION

É lógico que + (phrase with Subjunctive)**?**	Is it logical that ... ?
Acha lógico que + (phrase with Subjunctive)**?**	Do you think/find it logical that ... ?
Portanto ...	Therefore ...
Por conseguinte ...	Therefore ...
Por consequência ...	As a consequence ...
É lógico que + (phrase with Subjunctive)	It is logical that ...
É de esperar que + (phrase with Present Subjunctive)	It is to be expected that ...
Era de esperar que + (phrase with Past Subjunctive)	It would be expected that ...
Não é lógico que + (phrase with Subjunctive)	It is not logical that ...
Não é de esperar que + (phrase with Present Subjunctive)	It is not to be expected that ...
Não era de esperar que + (phrase with Past Subjunctive)	It wouldn't be expected that ...
Não tem lógica nenhuma que + (phrase with Subjunctive)	There is no logic at all in that ...

– **Não é lógico que depois de tantas negociações se faça este investimento?**
Isn't it logical that at the end of so much negotiating we embark on
this investment?

– **Não, não acho nada lógico, porque não temos garantias e ainda
podemos perder muito dinheiro.**
I do not find it logical at all, because we have no guarantees and we
can still lose a lot of money.

– **Mas as companhias com quem lidamos são de renome, por conseguinte, é de esperar que o investimento seja seguro.**
But we are dealing with companies with good reputations and, therefore, it is to be expected that the investment is safe.

15.6 EXPRESSING LACK OF COMPREHENSION AND REQUESTING CLARIFICATION

Não percebo.	
Não compreendo.	I do not understand.
Não entendo.	
Não estou a compreender.[B]	
Não percebo/compreendo nada.	I do not understand at all.
Não percebo/entendo porque ...	I do not understand why ...

Pode(s) repetir?	Can you repeat it?
Pode(s) repetir mais devagar?	Can you repeat more slowly?

Pode(s) explicar melhor?	Can you explain?
Pode(s) esclarecer melhor?	Can you be clearer?

– **Desculpe, mas não compreendo o que me está a dizer. Pode repetir, por favor?**
I am sorry but I do not understand what you are telling me. Can you repeat it, please?

– **...**
...

– **Continuo a não perceber porque é que a encomenda não pode ser entregue hoje. Pode explicar melhor?**
I still do not understand why the order cannot be delivered today. Can you explain it better?

15.7 STATING CERTAINTY OR UNCERTAINTY

Tenho a certeza.	I am sure.
Tenho a certeza de que ...	I am sure that ...
Estou certo/a de que ...	
Estou seguro/a de que ...	I am certain that ...
Não tenho a certeza.	I am not sure.
Não tenho a certeza de que + (phrase with Subjunctive)	I am not sure that ...
Não estou certo de que + (phrase with Subjunctive)	I am not certain that ...
Duvido que + (phrase with Subjunctive)	I doubt that ...

- **A Joana já terá enviado a encomenda?**
I wonder whether Joana has already sent the parcel?

- **Duvido. Ela disse que não estava certa se a poderia mandar anteontem ou na próxima semana.**
I doubt it. She said she was not sure whether she would be able to send it the day before yesterday or next week.

- **Estou certa de que não vai esperar pela próxima semana. Ela sabe como é urgente.**
I am sure she is not going to wait until next week. She knows how urgent it is.

- **Disso eu já não estou tão segura. Sabes como ela é esquecida.**
Of that I am not so sure. You know how forgetful she is.

- **Tens a certeza? Ela sempre me pareceu uma pessoa muito organizada.**
Are you sure? She has always struck me as a very organized person.

16 JUDGEMENT AND EVALUATION

16.1 EXPRESSING PLEASURE WITH OR LIKING OF SOMETHING OR SOMEONE

Prefiro ...	I prefer ...
Gosto de ...	I like ...
Adoro ...	I love ...
Que bom!	How nice!
Que bom que + (phrase with Subjunctive)	How nice that ...
Ainda bem que ...	It is good that ...
Estou satisfeito/a por + (phrase with Infinitive)	I am glad that ...
Estou satisfeito/a que + (phrase with Subjunctive)	I am glad that ...
Estou encantado/a por + (phrase with Infinitive)	I am delighted that ...
Estou encantado/a que + (phrase with Subjunctive)	I am delighted that ...
Tenho prazer em + (phrase with Infinitive)	I am pleased to ...
Tenho o prazer de[1] **+** (phrase with Infinitive)	I am pleased to ...
Muito prazer.[1]	Pleased to meet you.
Encantado/a.[1]	Delighted to meet you.

[1] Formulas used in introductions and presentations (see 12.9).

– **Estou encantada por terem vindo. Tenho tanto prazer em os conhecer.**
   I am delighted you came. I am so pleased to meet you.

– **Nós também estamos muito satisfeitos por nos encontrarmos final-mente. Adoramos conhecer outros ramos da família.**
   We are also very pleased to finally meet you. We love to meet other branches of the family.

– **Ainda bem que vieram hoje, porque assim também podem ter o prazer de conhecer a minha sogra, que está cá de visita.**
   It is good that you could come today because you can also have the pleasure of meeting my mother-in-law, who is spending some time with us.

16.2   EXPRESSING DISPLEASURE OR DISLIKE

Não gosto.	I do not like it.
Não gosto muito de ...	I am not very fond of ...
Não gosto nada.	I do not like it at all.
Não gosto nada que +	I hate that ...
(phrase with Subjunctive)	
Detesto!	I hate it!
Que mau gosto!	What horrid taste!
Que horror!	How dreadful!
É horroroso!	It is horrid/dreadful!
É horrível.	It is dreadful/horrible.
É horrível que +	It is dreadful that ...
(phrase with Subjunctive)	
Aborrece-me que +	It upsets me that ...
(phrase with Subjunctive)	
Estou aborrecido/a por +	I am upset because ...
(phrase with Infinitive)	

Irrita-me que + (phrase with Subjunctive) It irritates me that ...
Embirro que + (phrase with Subjunctive) It annoys me that ...
Detesto que + (phrase with Subjunctive)⎤
Odeio que + (phrase with Subjunctive) ⎦ I hate that ...

- **Que coisa horrorosa!**
  What a horrid thing!

- **O que é?**
  What is it?

- **É a prenda de Natal que a tia Aldegundes me mandou. É um pavor de mau gosto!**
  The Christmas present aunt Aldegundes sent me. It is the height of bad taste.

- **Realmente é um chapéu horrível. Onde é que se pode usar uma coisa dessas?**
  It really is a dreadful hat. Where can one wear anything like that?

- **Embirro que me mandem prendas estúpidas e inúteis. Detesto aquela tia.**
  I hate to be sent stupid and useless presents. I hate that aunt.

- **Eu também não gosto muito dela. Que prenda terá para mim?**
  I am not very fond of her either. What present will she have for me?

16.3 ENQUIRING ABOUT PLEASURE/DISPLEASURE, LIKING/DISLIKE

Gosta(s)?	Do you like it?
Gosta(s) de ... ?	Do you like ... ?
Está(s) satisfeito?	Are you pleased?
Está(s) satisfeito com ... ?	Are you pleased with ... ?

Não gosta(s)?	Don't you like it?
Não gosta(s) de ... ?	Don't you like ... ?
Não está(s) satisfeito?	Aren't you pleased?
Não está(s) satisfeito com ... ?	Aren't you pleased with ... ?

– **Gostava de umas sandálias de Verão.**
I would like a pair of Summer sandals.

– **Prefere com ou sem salto?**
Do you prefer them with or without heel?

– **Prefiro com um pouco de salto, mas não quero demasiado alto.**
I prefer them with a bit of a heel, but not too high.

– **Está satisfeita com estas?**
Are you happy with these?

– **Sim, gosto bastante destas, mas estão um pouco apertadas.**
Yes, I quite like these, but they are a little tight.

– **E com estas não está satisfeita? São de cabedal muito macio.**
And what about these, aren't you happy with them? They are in very soft leather.

– **Sim, estas são confortáveis. E gosto deste estilo. Pode mandar embrulhar.**
Yes, these are comfortable. And I also like this style. You can have them wrapped for me.

16.4 ENQUIRING AND EXPRESSING INTEREST/ LACK OF INTEREST

Gosta(s) de ... ?	Do you like ... ?
Não gosta(s) de ... ?	Don't you like ... ?
Interessa-se/Interessas-te por ... ?	Are you interested in ... ?
Não se interessa por ... ?/Não te interessas por ...?	Aren't you interested in ... ?
Deseja(s) ... ?	Would you like ... ?
Não deseja(s) ... ?	Wouldn't you like ... ?

Interessa-te/lhe + (phrase with Infinitive)?	Would you be interested in … ?
Não te/lhe interessa + (phrase with Infinitive)?	Wouldn't you be interested in … ?

É interessante.	It is interesting.
Interesso-me por …	I am interested in …
Tenho interesse por …	I am keen on …
Tenho curiosidade por …	I am keen on/I am curious about …

Não é de interesse.	It is of no interest.
Não me interessa.	I am not interested.
Não me interessa nada.	I am not interested at all.
Não tenho qualquer interesse.	I am not interested in the least.

- **Bom dia. Estou interessado num livro sobre o Brasil.**
  Good morning. I am interested in a book on Brazil.

- **Deseja esse aqui? É muito interessante. Tem muitas informações sobre os melhores hotéis e restaurantes.**
  Would you like this one? It is very interesting. It has a lot of information on the best hotels and restaurants.

- **Esse tipo de livro não tem interesse para mim. Tenho muita curiosidade pela antropologia do Brasil.**
  I am not interested in that type of book. I am very keen on Brazilian anthropology.

- **E esse aí, não lhe interessa? É uma publicação da Universidade do Rio de Janeiro.**
  What about this one, wouldn't you be interested? It is a University of Rio publication.

- **Não, esse não me interessa nada. É uma edição muito antiga.**
  No, that one is of no interest at all. That edition is too old.

16.5   EXPRESSING SURPRISE

Que surpresa!	What a surprise!
Quem diria?!	Who would believe it?!
Não era de esperar!	It was not (to be) expected!
Não era de esperar que + (phrase with Subjunctive)	It was not (to be) expected that …

Meus Deus!	
Minha Nossa Senhora![B]	Good God!

- **Professor Lacerda, que surpresa! Não esperava nada vê-lo aqui.**
  Prof. Lacerda, what a surprise! I didn't expect to see you here.

- **É a Margarida Canavarro, não é? Do curso de '95?**
  You are Margarida Canavarro, aren't you? Class of '95?

- **Pois sou. Quem diria que o havia de encontrar aqui em Manchester.**
  Yes, I am. Who could tell that I would meet you here in Manchester.

- **Na realidade eu não era para estar aqui, mas resolvi vir a este congresso de Fonética.**
  In fact, I hadn't planned to come but at the last minute I decided to attend this conference on Phonetics.

16.6   EXPRESSING HOPE

Oxalá!	I hope so!
Oxalá + (phrase with Subjunctive)	I hope ...
Quem dera!	Wouldn't we like that!
Se Deus quiser.	God willing. All being well.
Deus permita que + (phrase with Subjunctive)	We hope to God that ...
Era bom que + (phrase with Subjunctive)	It would be nice if ...
Deus nos livre!	Heaven forbid!
Deus nos livre que + (phrase with Subjunctive)	Heaven forbid that ...

Note: Sentences expressing hope are equivalent to a wish and require a Subjunctive (see 7.3).

- **Oxalá façam boa viagem.**
  I hope you have a good journey.

- **Se Deus quiser não vai haver novidade.**
  Hopefully, there will be no problem.

- **Tenho tanto medo das viagens longas de noite. Deus permita que não haja um acidente.**
  I am so scared of long journeys by night. I hope to God there won't be any accidents.

- **Deus nos livre, mãe. Vai ver que vai tudo correr bem.**
  Heaven forbid, mother. Everything will be all right, you will see.

- **Quem dera!**
  I do hope so!

16.7 ENQUIRING ABOUT AND EXPRESSING SATIS-FACTION/DISSATISFACTION

Está(s) satisfeito?	Are you satisfied/pleased?
Ficaste/ficou satisfeito?	Were you pleased?
Agrada-te/lhe + (phrase with Infinitive)	Would you like to . . . ?

Estou satisfeito/a.	I am pleased/satisfied.
Estou satisfeito/a com . . .	I am pleased/satisfied with . . .
Fiquei satisfeito/a.	I was satisfied.
Fiquei satisfeito/a com . . .	I was satisfied by . . .

Estou contente.	I am happy/contented.
Estou contente com . . .	I am happy/contented with . . .
Fiquei contente.	I was happy.
Fiquei contente com . . .	I was happy with . . .
Não estou satsifeito/a.	I am not pleased.
Não estou satsifeito/a com . . .	I am not happy with . . .
Não estou nada satisfeito/a com . . .	I am not happy at all with . . .

– **O Sr. Dr. ficou satisfeito com o hotel que lhe reservámos?**
  Were you pleased with the room we booked for you, Sir?

– **Sim, fiquei relativamente satisfeito. O quarto era confortável, com todas as comodidades, agradou-me a situação, próximo do metropolitano, mas não fiquei nada contente com a conta.**
  Yes, I was reasonably pleased – the room was comfortable, with all facilities, I appreciated its nearness to the underground, but I was not at all happy with the bill.

16.8 EXPRESSING DISAPPOINTMENT

Estou desiludido/a com . . .	
Estou desapontado/a com . . .	I am disappointed with . . .
Estou decepcionado/a com . . .	

Fiquei desiludido/a com . . .	
Fiquei desapontado/a com . . .	I was disappointed with . . .
Fiquei decepcionado/a com . . .	

– **Estou muito desiludido com o hotel Ratz. Tem muita fama, mas a qualidade do serviço é fraca e as diárias são caras.**
  I am very disappointed with the Ratz Hotel. It has a good reputation, but the service is poor and the daily rates are high.

– **Da última vez que lá fiquei também fiquei desapontado com o restaurante. O serviço foi demorado e a comida veio fria.**
  The last time I stayed there I was also disappointed with the restaurant. The service was slow and the food was cold.

16.9   ENQUIRING ABOUT AND EXPRESSING WORRY OR FEAR

Está(s) preocupado/a?	Are you worried?
Está(s) nervoso/a?	Are you nervous?
Tens/Tem medo? **Está(s) com medo?** }	Are you afraid?
Estou preocupado/a.	I am worried.
Estou nervoso/a.	I am nervous/anxious.
Estou uma pilha de nervos.	I am a bag of nerves.
Fico uma pilha de nervos	I become a bag of nerves.
Tenho medo.	I am afraid.
Tenho medo de + (phrase with Infinitive)	I am afraid to ...
Tenho um terror medonho de + (phrase with Infinitive)	I am dreadfully scared of ...
Ai, que medo!	Gosh! I'm scared!
Que medo!	How frightening!
Que susto!	What a fright!
Estou a tremer de medo.	I am shaking with fear.
Estou gelado/a de medo.	I am frozen with fear.
Estou aterrorizado/a.	I am terrified.

– **Estou a tremer de medo!**
  I am shaking with fear!

– **Que aconteceu?**
  What happened?

– **Fui lá fora passear o cão e ouvi passos atrás de mim.**
  I went out to walk the dog and I heard footsteps behind me.

– **Ai, que medo! Eu tenho um terror medonho de andar na rua sozinha à noite.**
  Gosh, how frightening! I am dreadfully scared of going out at night all by myself.

– **Eu não costumo ter medo quando vou com o cão, mas desta vez fiquei gelada porque os passos vinham para aqui.**
  Usually I am not afraid when I go out with the dog, but this time I was frozen with fear because the footsteps were coming in this direction.

– **Não me digas isso, que fico uma pilha de nervos.**
  Don't say that or I'll be a bag of nerves.

16.10 ENQUIRING ABOUT AND EXPRESSING PREFERENCE

Prefere(s) ... ?	Do you prefer ... ?
Qual prefere(s)?	Which do you prefer?
Por qual tens/tem preferência?	Which would you prefer?
De qual gosta(s) mais?	Which do you like best?

Não prefere(s) ...?	Wouldn't you prefer ... ?
Não gosta(s) mais de ... ?	Wouldn't you like ... more?

Prefiro ...	I prefer ...
Tenho preferência por ...	I would prefer ...
Gosto mais de ...	I like ... best.

– **Boa tarde. Tem blusas de malha?**
Good afternoon. Have you got any knitted tops?

– **Prefere de lã ou de algodão?**
Do you prefer in wool or cotton?

– **Gosto mais de algodão.**
I like cotton best.

– **Tem preferência por manga curta ou comprida?**
Would you prefer short or long sleeves?

– **Prefiro de manga comprida.**
I prefer with long sleeves.

16.11 EXPRESSING GRATITUDE

Obrigado/a.	Thank you.
Muito obrigado/a.	Thank you very much.
Agradeço muito.	I am very grateful.
Estou muito grato/a.	I am very grateful.

Bem haja(s).	God bless.
Deus te/lhe pague.	God bless you.

– **Muito obrigado pela boleia.**
Thanks a lot for the lift.

– **Não tem de quê, eu é que agradeço a companhia.**
It was nothing. I am the one who is grateful for the company.

– **Não calcula o jeito que me deu, senão tinha perdido o comboio. Bem haja.**
You can't imagine how convenient it was, otherwise I would have missed the train. God bless you.

– **Igualmente.**
And you.

16.12   EXPRESSING SYMPATHY

Tenho pena.	I am sorry.
Tenho muita pena. ⎤	
Lamento muito. ⎦	I am very sorry.
Os meus pêsames.	My sympathy.
Sinceros pêsames.[1]	In deepest sympathy.

[1]   Formula used in sympathy messages.

– **Lamento muito que o teu marido não esteja cá por ocasião da morte da tua sogra. Conta comigo no que for necessário.**
I am very sorry your husband is not here on the passing away of your mother-in-law. You can count on me for any help.

– **Muito obrigada. Agradecia que me ajudasses a tratar da correspondência.**
Thanks. I would be grateful if you could help me with the correspondence.

– **Está aqui um cartão de pêsames que veio da Madeira: 'Sentimos muito a morte da D. Jacinta. Sinceros pêsames. Abel e Carolina Silva.**
Here is a sympathy card from Madeira: 'Our deepest sympathy on the passing away of Mrs (Correia).[1] Abel and Carolina Silva.'

[1]   We are assuming that the deceased lady was called Mrs Jacinta Correia (see 12.10.4).

16.13   EXPRESSING HAPPINESS AND UNHAPPINESS

Estou feliz por +	I am happy to ...
(phrase with Infinitive)	
Estou contente por +	I am happy to ...
(phrase with Infinitive)	
Estou radiante.	I am overjoyed.
Estou louco/a de alegria.	I am over the moon.

– **Estou louca de alegria – conseguimos comprar o apartamento que queríamos no Algarve.**
I am over the moon – we managed to buy the apartment we wanted in the Algarve.

– **Parabéns! Eu também fico muito contente por vocês.**
Congratulations! I am also very happy for you.

– **Mas ainda estou mais radiante por termos conseguido vender a nossa casa em Inglaterra.**
But I am even more overjoyed because we managed to sell our house in England.

16.14   APOLOGIZING

Desculpe.	I am sorry. I beg your pardon.
Perdão.	I beg your pardon.
Com licença.	Excuse me. With your permission.

– **Com licença. Deixem passar, por favor.**
Excuse me. Please let me through.

– **Desculpe, mas eu estava à frente.**
I am sorry, but I was ahead of you.

– **Perdão, a senhora não estava na bicha.** [B]
I beg your pardon, but you were not queuing up.

– **Ai isso é que estava. Estava ao lado deste cavalheiro.**
Of course I was. I was standing next to this gentleman.

16.15   ENQUIRING ABOUT AND EXPRESSING APPROVAL/DISAPROVAL

Acha(s) bem?	Do you approve?
Acha(s) mal?	Do you disapprove?
Concorda(s)?	Do you agree?

Não acha(s) bem?	Don't you approve?
Não acha(s) mal?	You do not disapprove?
Não concorda(s)?	Don't you agree?

Sim.	Yes.
Pois!	Quite!
Pois claro.	Of course.
Sim senhor!	Well done!
Muito bem.	Very well. Well done.
Parabéns!	Congratulations!
Bravo!	Bravo!

Não.	No.
Não senhor!	Absolutely not.
Claro que não.	Of course not.
Não pode ser.	It can't be so.
Nunca!	Never!
Jamais!	Never ever!

Discordo.	I disagree.
Discordo plenamente.	I absolutely disagree.

– **Então fica acordado um investimento na ETC da ordem dos 500 mil contos. Acha bem?**
We then agree upon an investment of Esc.500 million in ETC. Do you approve?

– **Claro que não. Eu discordo plenamente.**
Of course not. I absolutely disagree.

– **Mas, na última reunião, o Sr. Director sugeriu que se fizesse um investimento na ETC ...**
But at our last meeting you advised that we should make an investment in ETC ...

– **Pois fiz, mas não de 500 mil contos.**
Quite! But not of Esc.500 million.

– **Então o Sr. Director acha mal?**
Do you disapprove, then?

– **Pois claro que acho! Eu aconselhei um pequeno investimento inicial, atendendo à insistência dos outros membros do conselho directivo.**
Of course I do! I advised a small initial investment, owing to the insistence of the other members of the Board.

– **Não senhor! O Sr. Director falou num investimento considerável.**
No, you didn't! You spoke of a considerable investment.

– **Eu? Naquela firma? Nunca!**
Me? In that firm? Never!

16.16 EXPRESSING APPRECIATION

Muito bem.	Very well.
Muito bom.	Very good.
Excelente.	Excellent.
Muito bonito.	Very pretty.
Que bonito!	How beautiful!
Maravilhoso.	Marvellous.
Extraordinário.	Outstanding.

– **Já esteve em Sintra?**
Have you already been to Sintra?

– **Ainda não. É bonito?**
No. Is it nice?

– **É lindo. O Palácio da Vila e o Palácio da Pena são extraordinária-
mente interessantes, e a paisagem da serra é maravilhosa.**
It is beautiful. The Palácio da Vila and the Pena Palace are extremely
interesting and the view of the mountain is wonderful.

– **Muito bem, então vou já marcar lugar numa excursão.**
Great! Then, I am going to book a seat on a tour straight away.

16.17   EXPRESSING REGRET

Lamento, mas ...	I am sorry but ...
Lamento muito.	I am very sorry.
Estou arrependido/a de + (phrase with Infinitive)	I regret ...
Se eu soubesse + (phrase with Imperfect or Conditional)	If I had known ...
Se pudesse voltar atrás + (phrase with Imperfect or Conditional)	If I could turn back time ...

– **Estou tão arrependido de ter ido a Sintra.**
I regret so much having gone to Sintra.

– **A sério? Porquê?**
Really? Why?

– **Porque caí duma muralha no Castelo dos Mouros e parti um pé.**
Because I fell from a wall in the Moors' Castle and broke my foot.

– **Não diga. Se eu soubesse não o tinha encorajado a lá ir.**
You don't say. If I had known, I wouldn't have encouraged you to go.

– **Pois é. Se pudesse voltar atrás tinha antes ido à praia.**
Quite. If I could turn back time, I would have gone to the beach
instead.

16.18   EXPRESSING INDIFFERENCE

Não tem importância.	It doesn't matter. Never mind.
Não tem importância nenhuma.	It doesn't matter at all.
Tanto faz.	It makes no difference.
É-me indiferente.	It's all the same to me.
Não me importa.	I don't mind.
Não me importa nada.	I don't mind at all.
Não me rala nada.	I do not care a bit.

- **Prefere carne ou peixe?**
  Do you prefer meat or fish?

- **Tanto faz.**
  It makes no difference.

- **E para beber? Prefere vinho branco ou tinto?**
  And to drink? Do you prefer white or red wine?

- **É-me indiferente.**
  It's all the same to me.

- **Nesse caso, importa-se que eu escolha?**
  In that case, do you mind if I choose?

- **Não me importa nada. Recebi a conta do hospital e perdi o apetite.**
  I don't mind at all. I received the hospital bill and lost my appetite.

- **Isso não tem importância. Vai ver que amanhã já está melhor.**
  Never mind. You will see that tomorrow you will feel better.

16.19   ACCUSING

Foste tu que ...	
Foi você/o senhor/a senhora que ... ⎫	It was you who ...
A culpa é tua/sua.	It is your fault.
A culpa é toda tua/sua.	It is all your fault.
Tu és o/a culpado/a de ... ⎫	You are to blame for ...
Você/o senhor é o culpado de ... ⎭	You are the culprit of ...

- **O senhor não vê por onde vai?**
  Can't you see where you are going?

- **Eu? O senhor é que bateu no meu carro.**
  Me? It was you who hit my car.

- **Não senhor. O senhor é que é o culpado deste acidente.**
  Not at all. You are to blame for this accident.

- **Perdão, mas a culpa é toda sua. Devia ter parado.**
  I beg your pardon, but it is all your fault. You should have stopped.

- **Desculpe, mas foi o senhor que entrou no cruzamento sem olhar.**
  Excuse me, but it was you who entered the junction without looking.

16.20 ENQUIRING ABOUT AND EXPRESSING CAPABILITY/INCAPABILITY

Sabe(s) + (phrase with Infinitive)**?**
Can you/Do you know how to ... ?

Pode(s) + (phrase with Infinitive)**?**
Can you ... ?

É(s) capaz de + (phrase with Infinitive)**?**
Can you/Are you capable of ... ?

Tens/Tem coragem de + (phrase with Infinitive)**?**
Have you got the courage to ...

Sei + (phrase with Infinitive)
I can/know how to ...

Posso + (phrase with Infinitive)
I can ...

Sou capaz de + (phrase with Infinitive)
I am capable of ...

Tenho coragem de + (phrase with Infinitive)
I have the courage to ...

Não sei + (phrase with Infinitive)
I cannot/don't know how to ...

Não sou capaz de + (phrase with Infinitive)
I cannot ...

Sou incapaz de + (phrase with Infinitive)
I am incapable of ...

Não tenho coragem de + (phrase with Infinitive)
I do not have the courage to ...

Não posso + (phrase with Infinitive)
I can't ...

– **Posso entrar?**
Can I come in?

– **Podes. Entra!**
Yes, please do.

– **És capaz de me dar uma ajuda?**
Can you give me a hand?

– **Claro, se puder.**
Of course, if I can.

– **Como sabes falar alemão, és capaz de me traduzir esta carta?**
As you know how to speak German, can you translate this letter?

– **Agora não posso. Tenho muito que fazer. Talvez à hora do almoço. Pode ser?**
At the moment I can't. I am too busy. Perhaps at lunch time. Is that all right?

PART III: BRAZILIAN VARIANTS

B1–11 BRAZILIAN ESSENTIAL GRAMMAR

Entries in this part refer only to variants found in Brazilian Portuguese. The numbering corresponds to those points marked with ^B in Parts I and II. Entries in this section are thus preceded by the prefix 'B'.

B12–16 LANGUAGE FUNCTIONS

As second person pronouns are seldom used in Brazilian Portuguese, remember to transform the examples in Part II into sentences with the verb in the third person, usually preceded by **você**, **vocês** or **o senhor**, **a senhora**, **os senhores**, **as senhoras** or any other subject. Many examples already illustrate the use of the third person, but, obviously, not all of them, as second person pronouns and verbal forms can be useful in other parts of the Portuguese-speaking world, even in some areas of Brazil.

Also, do not forget that Brazilian Portuguese Imperative forms are usually borrowed from the Present Subjunctive (see B7.4.1); therefore, examples with 'true' Imperatives using a second person must be transformed into sentences with the polite Imperative deriving from the Present Subjunctive.

B1 PRONUNCIATION AND SPELLING

PORTUGUESE VARIANTS AND SPELLING

There are some pronunciation and spelling variations among European Portuguese, Brazilian and even African Portuguese. These, however, are not wide enough to prevent communication. Needless to say that another important contributing factor towards variation within Portuguese is the inevitable lexical preference displayed by speakers of each area or country.

It is interesting to note that African Portuguese, especially the Portuguese spoken in Angola and Mozambique, seems to sit roughly in the middle of the variation spectrum between European and Brazilian Portuguese. There are historical factors which explain this, but they do not fall within the scope of an 'essential grammar' such as the present work. African Portuguese is understood to be the Portuguese spoken in the PALOP countries (**Países Africanos de Língua Oficial Portuguesa**), Angola, Cape Verde, Guinea-Bissau, Mozambique and S. Tomé e Príncipe – all former Portuguese colonies which became independent after 1974 and which adopted Portuguese as their official language.

The term 'African Portuguese' is by definition a wide generalization, as wide as Brazilian Portuguese. When considering such vast countries and continents there is bound to be a reasonable degree of variation from area to area. Variation is also patent in the various regions of a country as small as Portugal, although, as stated above, that should not hinder communication.

Spelling also reflects this variation. A number of orthographic agreements have been signed, the latest in 1992, trying, with varying degrees of success, to bring together the spelling adopted by the different Portuguese-speaking countries. This, however, will only come into force after having been approved in the respective parliaments of all signataries, which may only happen some years hence. In any case, most printed material in Portuguese, presently in circulation, follows the guidelines established by the 1973 agreement and considerable time will elapse before these are out-numbered by new publications adopting the 1992 orthographic agreement. For that reason, it was decided that the present work should follow the 1973 guidelines. Indeed, many Portuguese and Brazilian native speakers vow to maintain the present orthography, as that is the one they are used to. In all likelihood, the 1992 agreement will only be fully implemented and used with the new generation which is now entering primary school.

In general terms, the main concern of the 1992 agreement was to simplify and bring closer together the spelling adopted in all Portuguese-speaking countries but, at the same time, enabling it to reflect more closely the actual pronunciation used in each. For example, at the moment, the word **jacto** 'jet' is spelt with a **c** in European Portuguese but simply **jato** in the Brazilian variant, although the pronunciation is the same in both cases. When the 1992 agreement comes into force, the **c** will also disappear in European Portuguese spelling.

The case of words like **recepção** 'reception' is different. At present, the same spelling is adopted in all Portuguese-speaking countries; however, after the 1992 orthographic agreement comes into force, the **p** will be maintained in Brazilian Portuguese, because it is clearly pronounced there, but it will disappear in European Portuguese, because it is not pronounced in Portugal. The same will happen to the word **excepcional** 'exceptional' and a few others. Curiously, the word **excepção** 'exception' has a slightly different story. Whereas in European Portuguese it will also lose the **p**, in Brazilian Portuguese it has already been dropped because it is not pronounced.

Words such as **facto** 'fact' will maintain the **c** in European Portuguese, whereas in Brazil it has already been removed, hence **fato**, as the **c** is not pronounced there.

None of this should worry the learner unduly, because it is not of crucial importance at this stage, and orthography in all countries is going through a period of transition. Nor is the number of words affected, amongst the most commonly used terms for basic communication, significant enough to cause concern to the beginner, or even the intermediate-level student.

Therefore, and to generalize, the main difference in terms of orthography or spelling, when the 1992 agreement comes into force, is that the **c** or **p** before a consonant (**c**, **ç** or **t**) which is a remnant of the Portuguese Latin root, will be maintained if pronounced and omitted if not pronounced. There are also some modifications regarding hyphenation but these are best dealt with using an updated dictionary, which is good advice, anyway, when learning a new language.

In this essential grammar we have tried, as far as possible, to keep away from 'controversial' words and examples, as our objective is to provide the user with a brief, clear and neutral manual which, above all, stresses the general rule more than the exception, and the common ground of the various Portuguese variants, rather than their idiosyncrasies.

PRONUNCIATION

The two main differences in patterns of pronunciation between Brazilian and European Portuguese lie in the tendency to open most vowels in the former and a difference in rhythm or intonation. Brazilian Portuguese is more musical and uses fewer fricative sounds, as the final **s** is usually pronounced as 's' or 'z' instead of 'sh' or 'j' as in the European variant.

European Portuguese may sound a little harsher to the beginner because of the more strongly marked contrast between the open vowels in the stressed syllable and the closed and unvoiced vowels in unstressed and final syllables.

Some vowels and consonants are pronounced differently depending on their position in the word, as we point out below.

B1.1   VOWELS

B1.1.1   Oral vowels

		Example	*Pronounced as*
e	in final position	**cheque**	shak*y*
o	stressed **o** before **m** or **n**	**Antônio**	t*oo*k

B1.2   CONSONANTS

d	before **i**, or **e** when pronounced as **i**	**verda*d*e** **d̃ia**	*genie* *geography*
l	final position = diphthongs **au, éu, iu**	**Portuga*l*** **ca*l*ções** **pape*l*** **funi*l***	w*ow* c*ou*ch (see 1.1.1) *Eu*rope
s	at end of syllable/word if followed by unvoiced consonant (**t, c, f, p,**)	**e*s*tou** **mo*s*ca** **fó*s*foros** **meu*s* pais**	touri*st* mo*s*que pho*s*phor ve*s*pers
	at end of syllable/word if followed by voiced consonant (**b, d, g, m, n, r**)	**Li*s*boa** **ra*s*gar** **mai*s* dá** **me*s*mo** **ci*s*ne** **I*s*rael**	Li*s*bon let'*s* go Dre*s*den me*s*merize O*s*nabruck I*s*rael
t	before **i**, or **e** when pronounced as **i**	**t̃io** **pen*t*e**	*ch*eek pea*ch*y
z	final	**lu*z***	lo*ss*

B1.3   DIPHTHONGS

B1.3.2   Nasal diphthongs

Brazilian nasal diphthongs seem to have more nasal resonance than their European Portuguese equivalents.

B2 NOUNS

B2.4 DIMINUTIVES AND AUGMENTATIVES

B2.4.1 Diminutives are used more frequently in Brazilian Portuguese than in other variants.

B2.4.3 Brazilian Portuguese favours *diminutives* in **-inho** and **-zinho** in preference to **-ito**.

B3 ARTICLES

B3.2 USE OF THE DEFINITE ARTICLE

B3.2.1 With first names

In Brazilian Portuguese the use of the definite article is optional with fore-names and surnames, especially if referring to some well-known personality:

João disse que vinha mais tarde.
João said he was coming later.

O Nelson chega amanhã.
Nelson arrives tomorrow.

Jorge Amado é dos autores brasileiros mais conhecidos.
Jorge Amado is one of the best-known Brazilian writers.

B3.2.2 With titles

The definite article is frequently omitted before the title **D. (dona)**.

D. Margarida já saiu.   Mrs ... has already left.

B3.2.5 Before possessive adjectives

The definite article is also frequently omitted before possessive adjectives:

Nosso carro quebrou.   Our car has broken down.

B4 ADJECTIVES

B4.3. DEGREE

B4.3.3 Special comparative and superlative forms

In Brazilian Portuguese, **menor** 'smaller' is the correct comparative for **pequeno** 'small'. The equivalent superlative relative is **o menor**.

B5 PRONOUNS

B5.1 PERSONAL PRONOUNS

B5.1.1 Subject pronouns

Tu and **vós** are hardly ever used in Brazil. They have been superseded by **você**, **vocês**, **o senhor** and its variants **a senhora**, **os senhores**, **as senhoras**. **Tu** may be used in some regions of the south and the northeast of Brazil, sometimes as an indefinite subject such as 'one', 'anyone', 'a person'. If used, it is frequently combined with a verbal form in the third person singular, instead of second person. This is an extremely colloquial use of the pronoun and, as it is grammatically incorrect, it should be avoided.

Tu vai ao banco e todo mundo quer saber.
You go to the bank and everybody wants to know about it.

B5.1.1.1 As a rule, personal pronouns are more frequently used in Brazilian Portuguese than in European Portuguese.

B5.1.2 Direct object pronouns

Vos is hardly ever used in Brazil. **Vocês** is the preferred form. **O senhor**, **a senhora**, **os senhores**, **as senhoras** can also be used as direct object pronouns. **Te** (singular only) is used as a direct object in colloquial speech referring back to **você**:

Ela viu vocês no teatro.
She saw you at the theatre.

Eles convidaram os senhores para jantar.
They have invited you for dinner.

Nós te procuramos lá, mas você não nos viu.
We looked for you there but you didn't see us.

B5.1.2.1 In Brazilian Portuguese, direct object pronouns follow roughly the same norms as in European Portuguese, but they enjoy far greater freedom in matters of word order.

(e) *With single infinitives* it is possible to place the pronoun after the verb, even in a negative sentence:

Para não incomodá-lo mais ela preferiu se calar.
In order not to upset him further, she decided to be quiet.

(f) *In phrases where a main verb is used as an auxiliary* the pronoun can also come after the main verb of the sentence, be it in the Infinitive or Present Participle, even if it is a negative sentence:

Ela não queria vê-lo mais.
She didn't want to see him again.

(g) *In phrases where a main verb is used as an auxiliary* it is also possible to place the pronoun before the main verb in the sentence/clause, usually an Infinitive:

Eles querem nos-ver imediatamente.
They want to see us immediately.

(h) *In compound tenses* it is also possible to place the pronoun before the main verb, usually a Participle:

As crianças tinham se perdido no centro da cidade.
The children had got lost in the centre of town.

(i) *When two or more verbs share the same subject pronoun*, the pronoun only needs to be stated once, followed by the verbs:

Heitor a encontrou e levou para casa.
Heitor found it and took it home.

B5.1.2.3 *With Future and Conditional tenses* it is possible to place the pronoun before the verb in main affirmative sentences instead of fitting it between the stem and the ending, as is the norm in European Portuguese:

Nós o receberemos com muito gosto.
We will receive it with pleasure.

Rita nos reconheceria em qualquer lugar.
Rita would recognize us anywhere.

B5.1.3   Indirect object pronouns

These follow roughly the same norms as direct object pronouns. **Vos** is hardly ever used in Brazil. **Vocês** is the preferred form but in this case it needs to be introduced by a preposition. The same applies to **o senhor**, **a senhora**, **os senhores**, **as senhoras**, used in more formal circumstances. **Te** (singular only) is used as an indirect object in colloquial speech and refers back to **você**:

Quem deu esse presente para você?
Who gave you that present?

Eu escrevi uma carta para vocês.
I have written a letter to you.

O empregado dá a chave do quarto aos senhores.
The attendant gives you the bedroom key.

Não te disse que ela vinha?
Didn't I tell you she would come?

B5.1.5   Prepositional pronouns

Ti, **si** and **vós** are hardly ever used in Brazil. **Você** and **vocês** are the preferred equivalent forms:

Tenho um presente para você.   I have a present for you.
Tenho presentes para vocês.   I have presents for you.

B5.1.6   Reflexive pronouns

These follow roughly the same norms as direct object pronouns. **Te** and **vos** are seldom used in Brazil. **Se** is the preferred equivalent form in both cases as it corresponds to third person singular and plural:

Você se preocupa em demasia.   You worry too much.
Vocês se levantam muito cedo.   You get up very early.

B5.2   POSSESSIVE PRONOUNS AND ADJECTIVES

In Brazilian Portuguese, the definite article is frequently omitted before possessive adjectives; but there is a preference for using the definite article with possessive pronouns, especially in structures containing the verb **ser** and when emphasis is on an item one wishes to distinguish from another:

Possessive adjective	*Possessive pronoun*
Minhas **malas são pesadas.**	**As malas pesadas são** *as minhas* **(não as leves).**
My suitcases are heavy.	The heavy suitcases are mine (not the light ones).

Note: **As malas pesadas são minhas**, without the definite article, makes the same statement but without stressing that it is the heavy cases, as opposed to the light ones.

B5.2.1   Possessive adjectives

(O) teu, **(a) tua**, **(os) teus**, **(as) tuas** and especially **(o) vosso**, **(a) vossa**, **(os) vossos**, **(as) vossas** are seldom used in Brazil. **(O) seu**, **(a) sua**, **(os) seus**, **(as) suas** are the preferred equivalent forms and correspond to the personal pronouns **você, vocês**. In a colloquial register, it is also possible to use **de você, de vocês** as possessive adjectives.

Sua filha é muito simpática.
Your daughter is very nice.

Vocês sairam com seus amigos.
You went out with your friends.

B5.2.2   Possessive pronouns

O teu, a tua, os teus, as tuas and **o vosso, a vossa, os vossos, as vossas** are seldom used in Brazil. **O seu, a sua, os seus, as suas** are the preferred equivalent forms and correspond to the personal pronouns **você, vocês**. In a colloquial register, it is also possible to use **o/a/os/as de você, o/a/os/as de vocês**.

Essa mala é a sua (não aquela).
This is your suitcase (not the other one). (selection)

Essas malas são nossas, mas aquelas são as de vocês.
These suitcases are ours but *those are yours*. (selection)

Essas malas são nossas, mas aquelas são de vocês.
These suitcases are ours but those are yours. (possession only)

B6 NUMERALS

B.6.1 CARDINAL, ORDINAL AND MULTIPLICATIVE NUMBERS

As a rule these coincide in all variants of Portuguese, but in Brazilian Portuguese, some cardinals are written differently:

14	quatorze *or* catorze
16	dezesseis
17	dezessete
19	dezenove

B7   VERBS

The main difference between Brazilian Portuguese and other variants of the language is that in Brazil 'true' second person verbal forms are seldom used, because, as seen above (B5.1.1), **tu** and **vós** have been replaced by **você** and **vocês** (also **o senhor, a senhora, os senhores, as senhoras**) which require verbal forms in the third person. Some modern grammars and language courses in Brazilian Portuguese as a foreign language have even ceased to register second person verbal forms.

B7.4   IMPERATIVE MOOD

B7.4.1   Conjugation

In Brazilian Portuguese, as subject pronouns **tu** and **vós** are seldom used (see B5.1.1), all forms of the Imperative are borrowed from the Present Subjunctive.

B7.6   PRESENT PARTICIPLE

Estar + Present Participle is the preferred form for Progressive tenses:

Eu estava trabalhando quando você me interrompeu.
I was working when you disturbed me.

B7.12   REFLEXIVE VERBS

As second person pronouns are seldom used in Brazilian Portuguese (B5.1.1, B5.1.6, B7), second person forms are also seldom used with these verbs.

B7.12.1.2   In Brazilian Portuguese it is possible to attach the possessive pronoun to the beginning of the main verb in the Infinitive (see B5.1.2.1g):

Posso me sentar aqui?   Can I sit here?

B7.12.1.3   In Brazilian Portuguese, with Future and Conditional tenses, it is possible to place the pronoun before the verb in main positive sentences instead of fitting it between the stem and the ending, as is the norm in European Portuguese (see B5.1.2.3):

Eles se arrependerão disso.
They will regret it.

As crianças se cansariam muito depressa.
The children would soon be tired.

Note: Although the Conditional is used more frequently in Brazilian Portuguese than in the European variant of the language, the Future is extremely rare.

B10 PREPOSITIONS

B10.4 VERBS FOLLOWED BY A PREPOSITION

In Brazilian Portuguese **ir em** is preferred when expressing place being visited, usually a local place:

Este Verão eu vou em Araxá.
I am going to Araxá this Summer.

(*also* **pra Araxá** which is rather colloquial)

B11 ADDITIONAL NOTES ON BRAZILIAN PORTUGUESE USAGE

B11.1 GENTE/A GENTE

In colloquial Brazilian Portuguese **gente** can also mean 'you folks'. But remember that it cannot be used as a pronoun – it is a vocative:

Ele fez isso de propósito, gente.
He did that on purpose, folks.

B11.4 A/PARA

In Brazilian Portuguese the preposition **em**, in colloquial speech, can convey both meanings.

Eu vou em São Paulo em viagem de negócios.
(and I am coming back soon)

Eu vou em São Paulo.
(one assumes that I do not know when I will be back)

Note: It is also possible to say **para**.

B11.12 WORD ORDER

B11.12.1 Pronouns and verbs

In Brazilian Portuguese word order norms for object pronouns are not as rigid as in European Portuguese (see above, B5.1.2.1):

Ela *me* telefonou e escreveu uma carta.
She phoned *me* and sent me a letter.

Ela tinha *me* escrito uma carta.
She had sent *me* a letter.

Ela *me* escreverá uma carta.[1]
She will send *me* a letter.

Ela *me* escreveria uma carta.
She would send *me* a letter.

[1] This example is only for purposes of illustration, as the Future Tense is seldom used in Brazilian Portuguese (see B7.12.1.3).

B12 SOCIALIZING

B12.2. TAKING LEAVE

B12.2.1 Informal

Até logo in Brazilian Portuguese has the same meaning as an informal 'goodbye'. Brazilians use this expression even when they know they are not going to meet later in the day.

Tchau! also occurs in colloquial speech meaning 'Bye!/Cheerio!'

B12.2.1.1 For other leave-taking formulas, see information in 12.2.1.1.

B12.4 ATTRACTING ATTENTION

Por favor is preferred in Brazil instead of **faça favor**.
Garçon! is the usual way to call 'Waiter!'

B12.10 FORMS OF ADDRESS

In Brazil, the most widely used form of address is **você** and **vocês**. Brazilians use **você** to the extent of mixing it with other forms of address in the same sentence:

> **D. Lina, tenho um presentinho para você.**

or

> **D. Lina, tenho um presentinho para a senhora.**
> Mrs ... I have a little present for you.

The impact of **você** is so great that a few years ago a Brazilian president gave a good dressing down to a journalist who first addressed him as **Senhor Presidente** and then allowed a **você** to slip through, instead of using **Vossa Excelência** for a pronoun, as was required.

Tu is seldom used, only in some regions by certain sectors of the population, and is often incorrectly combined with verbal forms in the third person, as people regard **tu** as more informal, but are not used to employing a verbal form in the second person singular (see B5.1.1). As stated above, this use should be avoided.

Vós is even more rarely used, and is almost exclusively a form of address reserved for God in one's prayers.

B12.10.2   Less informal

In Brazilian Portuguese it is not possible to use the name of the person being spoken to as a subject pronoun, as is frequently the case in European Portuguese. A Brazilian, on being addressed by his/her own name, will instinctively think that the speaker is referring to someone else who happens to have the same name. As **você** is widely accepted as a form of address for most people, except on formal occasions, it does not need to be avoided and a speaker of Brazilian Portuguese does not need to find other alternatives, as a European speaker would in the same circumstances.

Nevertheless, when wishing to address someone amidst a group of people, the way to single that person out is to use the name as a vocative and then continue with the sentence or question desired, using **você** as the subject:

> **Carlos, você já viu esse filme?**
> Carlos, have you already seen that film?

> **Francisco e Daniela, como vocês estão de visita, não querem vir também?**
> Francisco and Daniela, as you are here on a visit, wouldn't you like to come too?

In a colloquial register, if **o senhor** is being used in front of a forename, it can assume the form of **seu**:

> – **Seu Juca, que surpresa encontrar o senhor por aqui.**
> Mr ... what a surprise to meet you here.

> – **É verdade seu Tristão.**
> That's right, Mr ...

B12.10.3   Formal

In Brazilian Portuguese **o senhor** and the variants, **a senhora, os senhores, as senhoras** are the other most current forms of expressing a second person subject, in this case with more formal overtones. These can also be used as object pronouns.

Senhorita 'Miss' can be used as a title for single (unmarried) women, but usually in a formal register. It is rarely used in spoken Portuguese and can have pejorative overtones. Unlike European Portuguese, in Brazilian Portuguese **a menina** cannot be used as a title for a single (unmarried) woman. The same applies to **o menino**, **a menina**, **os meninos**, **as meninas** even if one wishes to address children. **Você**, **vocês** would be the preferred forms.

Married and middle-aged women without a higher-education degree or a professional title are usually addressed as **Dona** followed by their first name.

Other ways of saying 'you': **Vossa Senhoria**, **(V.S.ª)** is still used in Brazil, although almost exclusively in formal letter writing, to address high-ranking civil servants and members of the forces, whereas in Portugal it has become obsolete.

B12.10.4   Titles

In general terms, titles in Brazilian Portuguese tend to coincide with usage in other Portuguese variants.

B12.10.5   Family

Brazilians prefer the following affectionate terms of address:

papai, mamãe	daddy, mummy
vovô, vovó	grandad, granny
titio, titia	uncle, auntie

Note: In Brazilian Portuguese none of these forms can be used as subjects, *only as vocatives*. If a subject or object pronoun is required, the preferred forms are **você(s)** and **o senhor**, **a senhora**, etc.:

- **Titio, nós gostávamos muito que o senhor e Titia viessem jantar em nossa casa.**
  Uncle ... we would like you and Auntie to come and have dinner at our house.

- **Pois não, Zeca, com muito gosto.**
  Of course, Zeca, we would be delighted.

B12.13   TALKING ABOUT THE WEATHER

As continuous tenses are built with the main verb in the Present Participle in Brazilian Portuguese, weather expressions requiring this sort of tense differ somewhat from European Portuguese:

Está chovendo.	It is raining.
Está nevando.	It is snowing.
Está trovejando.	There is a thunderstorm.
Está relampejando.	It is lightning.

Está fazendo sol.	The sun is shining.
Está ventando.	The wind is blowing.
Está fazendo frio.	It is rather cold.

– **Está fazendo muito frio aqui em São Paulo.**
  It is very cold here in São Paulo.

– **Eu não acho, você é que vem lá do Recife e não está habituado.**
  I don't think so, but as you come from Recife, you are not used to
  it.

B13 EXCHANGING FACTUAL INFORMATION

B13.3 ASKING FOR INFORMATION

As word order in Brazilian Portuguese can be far more flexible than in European Portuguese, especially in relation to object pronouns (see B5.1.2.1), some requests for information may present slightly different word order:

Pode me dizer ... (sentence with interrogative)?
Could you tell me ... ?

Me diga ... (sentence with interrogative), **por favor.**
Can you please tell me ... ?

Sabe me dizer ... (sentence with interrogative)?
Could you tell me ... ?

B13.5. LETTER WRITING

B13.5.1 Dates

In Brazilian Portuguese months are written in lower case:

Salvador, 30 de novembro de 1998
Salvador, 30 November 1998

B13.5.2 Opening formulas

B13.5.2.1 *Formal*: **Il$^{mo(a)}$ Senhor(a)** may be preferred in Brazilian Portuguese.

B14   GETTING THINGS DONE

B14.8   REQUESTING ASSISTANCE

As word order in Brazilian Portuguese can be far more flexible than in European Portuguese, especially in relation to object pronouns (see B5.1.2.1), some requests for assistance may present slightly different word order:

Me ajude a + (phrase with Infinitive)	Help me to ...
Pode me ajudar a + (phrase with Infinitive)?	Would you help me to ... ?
Me dê uma ajuda.	Give me a hand.

- **Me ajude a lavar o carro, por favor.**
  Help me wash the car, please.

- **Está bem, mas depois você também me dá uma ajudinha com o jardim.**
  All right, but afterwards you give me a hand in the garden too.

B15 FINDING OUT ABOUT AND EXPRESSING INTELLECTUAL ATTITUDES

B15.6 EXPRESSING LACK OF COMPREHENSION AND REQUESTING CLARIFICATION

As continuous tenses in Brazilian Portuguese are built with the main verb in the Present Participle, sentences explaining your present lack of clarification or state of confusion also require a Present Participle:

Não estou vendo nada.	I do not understand/see at all.
Não estou entendendo nada.	I do not understand a thing.
Não estou sabendo de nada.	I have not heard anything.

– **Aquilo foi tudo uma grande confusão, mas no fim tudo deu certo. Você está vendo?**
That was all a huge mess but in the end it all worked out all right. Do you see?

– **Não, eu não estou vendo nada. Você pode explicar melhor?**
No, I don't see it at all. Can you explain it better?

B16 JUDGEMENT AND EVALUATION

B16.5 EXPRESSING SURPRISE

Minha!/Nossa![1]	Oh, my!
Minha Nossa Senhora!	Golly! Gosh!

[1] These exclamations seem to be a short form of **Minha vida!** or **Minha Nossa Senhora!**

B16.14 APOLOGIZING

Fila is the correct word for 'queue' in Brazil.

BIBLIOGRAPHY

Alves, Manuel dos Santos, *Prontuário da língua portuguesa*, Lisbon: Livraria Popular de Francisco Franco, 1991.

Camara, J.R. and Mattoso, J., *The Portuguese Language* (English version by Anthony J. Naro), Chicago: Chicago University Press, 1972.

—— *História e estrutura da língua portuguesa*, Rio de Janeiro: Padrão – Livraria Editora, 1979.

Casteleiro, João Malaca, Meira, Américo and Pascoal, José, *Nível limiar: para o ensino [e] aprendizagem de português como língua segunda [e] língua estrangeira*, Strasburg: Conseil d'Europe, Lisbon: Instituto de Cultura e Língua Portuguesa, 1988.

Cintra, Luís F. Lindley, *Sobre 'Formas de tratamento' na língua portuguesa*, Lisbon: Livros Horizonte, 1986.

Corôa, Maria Luiza Monteiro Sales, *O tempo nos verbos do português: uma introdução à sua interpretação semântica*, Brasília: Thesaurus, 1985.

Cunha, Celso, *Gramática do português contemporâneo*, Belo Horizonte: Editora Bernardo Alvares, 1971.

Cunha, Celso and Cintra, Luís F. Lindley, *Nova gramática do português contemporâneo*, Lisbon: Edições João Sá da Costa, 1984.

Dias, Eduardo Mayone, Lathrop, Thomas A. and Rosa, Joseph G., *Portugal: língua e cultura*, Los Angeles: Cabrilho Press, 1977.

Ellison, Fred P. and Matos, Francisco Gomes de, *Modern Portuguese*, New York: Alfred A. Knopf, 1971.

Greenbaum, Sidney, *An Introduction to English Grammar*, London: Longman, 1991.

Leite, Isabel Coimbra and Coimbra, Olga Mata, *Português sem fronteiras*, Lisbon: Edições Técnicas, 1989.

Michael, Ian, *English Grammatical Categories*, Cambridge: Cambridge University Press, 1970.

Nogueira, Rodrigo de Sá, *Dicionário de verbos portugueses conjugados*, Lisbon: Livraria Clássica Editora, 1986.

Quirk, Randolph, Greenbaum, Sidney, Leech, Geoffrey and Svartvik, Jan, *A Comprehensive Grammar of the English Language*, New York: Longman, 1985.

Rodrigues, Fernando José and Humphreys, Peter, *Falar é aprender: português para estrangeiros*, Oporto: Porto Editora, 1993.

Willis, R.C., *An Essential Course in Modern Portuguese*, London: Harrap, 1971.

INDEX

This index includes: (a) grammatical terms which are used in the grammar or commonly used in reference grammars or descriptions of Portuguese; (b) English grammatical words such as 'whatever'; (c) words referring to language functions.

Note: Section number followed by a capital 'B' indicates that there is a corresponding item in **PART III: BRAZILIAN VARIANTS**.